OPPOSING VIEWPOINTS® SERIES

Native Americans

Other Books of Related Interest:

Opposing Viewpoints Series

Gambling

Interracial America

Population

Unemployment

Welfare

Introducing Issues with Opposing Viewpoints Series

Energy Alternatives

Global Viewpoints Series

Discrimination

Human Rights

Water

Current Controversies Series

US Government Corruption

"Congress shall make no law . . . abridging the freedom of speech, or of the press."

First Amendment to the US Constitution

The basic foundation of our democracy is the First Amendment guarantee of freedom of expression. The Opposing Viewpoints series is dedicated to the concept of this basic freedom and the idea that it is more important to practice it than to enshrine it.

OPPOSING VIEWPOINTS® SERIES

Native Americans

Lynn M. Zott, Book Editor

GREENHAVEN PRESS
A part of Gale, Cengage Learning

GALE
CENGAGE Learning·

Detroit • New York • San Francisco • New Haven, Conn • Waterville, Maine • London

Elizabeth Des Chenes, *Director, Publishing Solutions*

© 2012 Greenhaven Press, a part of Gale, Cengage Learning.

Gale and Greenhaven Press are registered trademarks used herein under license.

For more information, contact:
Greenhaven Press
27500 Drake Rd.
Farmington Hills, MI 48331-3535
Or you can visit our Internet site at gale.cengage.com

For product information and technology assistance, contact us at

Gale Customer Support, 1-800-877-4253
For permission to use material from this text or product, submit all requests online at www.cengage.com/permissions

Further permissions questions can be emailed to permissionrequest@cengage.com

Articles in Greenhaven Press anthologies are often edited for length to meet page requirements. In addition, original titles of these works are changed to clearly present the main thesis and to explicitly indicate the author's opinion. Every effort is made to ensure that Greenhaven Press accurately reflects the original intent of the authors. Every effort has been made to trace the owners of copyrighted material.

Cover Image copyright © Photosani/ShutterStock.com.

LIBRARY OF CONGRESS CATALOGING-IN-PUBLICATION DATA

Native Americans / Lynn M. Zott, book editor.
   p. cm. -- (Opposing viewpoints)
   Includes bibliographical references and index.
   ISBN 978-0-7377-5444-5 (hardback) -- ISBN 978-0-7377-5445-2 (paperback)
   1. Indians of North America--History--Juvenile literature. 2. Indians of North America--Social life and customs--Juvenile literature. I. Zott, Lynn M. (Lynn Marie), 1969-
   E77.4.N3834 2012
   970.004'97--dc23

                                      2011044654

Printed in the United States of America
1 2 3 4 5 6 7 16 15 14 13 12

Contents

**Chapter 3: How Do Disputes
over Resources and Artifacts Affect
Native Americans?**

Chapter 4: What Economic Factors Most Concern Native Americans?

Why Consider Opposing Viewpoints?

> *"The only way in which a human being can make some approach to knowing the whole of a subject is by hearing what can be said about it by persons of every variety of opinion and studying all modes in which it can be looked at by every character of mind. No wise man ever acquired his wisdom in any mode but this."*
>
> John Stuart Mill

In our media-intensive culture it is not difficult to find differing opinions. Thousands of newspapers and magazines and dozens of radio and television talk shows resound with differing points of view. The difficulty lies in deciding which opinion to agree with and which "experts" seem the most credible. The more inundated we become with differing opinions and claims, the more essential it is to hone critical reading and thinking skills to evaluate these ideas. Opposing Viewpoints books address this problem directly by presenting stimulating debates that can be used to enhance and teach these skills. The varied opinions contained in each book examine many different aspects of a single issue. While examining these conveniently edited opposing views, readers can develop critical thinking skills such as the ability to compare and contrast authors' credibility, facts, argumentation styles, use of persuasive techniques, and other stylistic tools. In short, the Opposing Viewpoints Series is an ideal way to attain the higher-level thinking and reading skills so essential in a culture of diverse and contradictory opinions.

In addition to providing a tool for critical thinking, Opposing Viewpoints books challenge readers to question their own strongly held opinions and assumptions. Most people form their opinions on the basis of upbringing, peer pressure, and personal, cultural, or professional bias. By reading carefully balanced opposing views, readers must directly confront new ideas as well as the opinions of those with whom they disagree. This is not to argue simplistically that everyone who reads opposing views will—or should—change his or her opinion. Instead, the series enhances readers' understanding of their own views by encouraging confrontation with opposing ideas. Careful examination of others' views can lead to the readers' understanding of the logical inconsistencies in their own opinions, perspective on why they hold an opinion, and the consideration of the possibility that their opinion requires further evaluation.

Evaluating Other Opinions

To ensure that this type of examination occurs, Opposing Viewpoints books present all types of opinions. Prominent spokespeople on different sides of each issue as well as well-known professionals from many disciplines challenge the reader. An additional goal of the series is to provide a forum for other, less known, or even unpopular viewpoints. The opinion of an ordinary person who has had to make the decision to cut off life support from a terminally ill relative, for example, may be just as valuable and provide just as much insight as a medical ethicist's professional opinion. The editors have two additional purposes in including these less known views. One, the editors encourage readers to respect others' opinions—even when not enhanced by professional credibility. It is only by reading or listening to and objectively evaluating others' ideas that one can determine whether they are worthy of consideration. Two, the inclusion of such viewpoints encourages the important critical thinking skill of objectively evaluating an author's credentials and bias. This evaluation will illuminate an author's reasons for taking a particular stance on an issue and will aid in readers' evaluation of the author's ideas.

It is our hope that these books will give readers a deeper understanding of the issues debated and an appreciation of the complexity of even seemingly simple issues when good and honest people disagree. This awareness is particularly important in a democratic society such as ours in which people enter into public debate to determine the common good. Those with whom one disagrees should not be regarded as enemies but rather as people whose views deserve careful examination and may shed light on one's own.

Thomas Jefferson once said that "difference of opinion leads to inquiry, and inquiry to truth." Jefferson, a broadly educated man, argued that "if a nation expects to be ignorant and free . . . it expects what never was and never will be." As individuals and as a nation, it is imperative that we consider the opinions of others and examine them with skill and discernment. The Opposing Viewpoints series is intended to help readers achieve this goal.

David L. Bender and Bruno Leone,
Founders

Introduction

> *"America's journey has been marked both by bright times of progress and dark moments of injustice for American Indians and Alaska Natives. Since the birth of America, they have contributed immeasurably to our country and our heritage, distinguishing themselves as scholars, artists, entrepreneurs, and leaders in all aspects of our society. Native Americans have also served in the United States armed forces with honor and distinction, defending the security of our nation with their lives. Yet, our tribal communities face stark realities, including disproportionately high rates of poverty, unemployment, crime, and disease. These disparities are unacceptable, and we must acknowledge both our history and our current challenges if we are to ensure that all of our children have an equal opportunity to pursue the American dream."*
>
> —President Barack Obama,
> "Presidential Proclamation on National
> Native American Heritage Month,"
> October 29, 2010.

"Don't get sick after June" is a phrase often repeated in discussions of the Indian Health Service (IHS), referencing the month by which federal funding for the program is exhausted each year. "American Indians have an infant death rate that is 40 percent higher than the rate for whites. They are twice as likely to die from diabetes, 60 percent more likely to have a stroke, 30 percent more likely to have high blood pressure and 20 percent more likely to have heart disease," according to Mary Clare Jalonick.[1] Revenue from casinos or other tribal-owned businesses enables some tribes to supplement the IHS-funded care, but for economically disadvantaged tribes, particularly those living on remote reservations, the disease statistics are grim. According to a report published by Novo Nordisk in November 2010,[2] the rate of diabetes among Native Americans is six times that of non-Hispanic whites in the United States; the report also cites statistics from the Indian Health Service's Division of Diabetes Treatment and Prevention that the rates of complications and death from diabetes are significantly higher than for the rest of the American population—Native Americans are 3.5 times more likely to suffer kidney damage and 3 times more likely to die as a result of diabetes.[3]

The greatest determinant of chronic health problems among Native American populations is reported to be poverty. According to the Novo Nordisk report, "the biggest contributor to the diabetes challenges facing Native Americans stem from simple economics. A high percentage of Native Americans live in poverty. Poorer communities are more likely to have unhealthy diets, reduced physical activity, higher rates of obesity, alcoholism, and emotional problems, and lack of access to adequate health education and services—factors that escalate the risks for chronic conditions like diabetes."[4] Statistics also indicate that the funding for the Indian Health Service is markedly lower than that of other federal health care programs. Figures for annual per-person expenditures on the IHS website for 2005 illustrate that the financing for Medicaid was $4,000 per person, for Medicare it was $7,000 per person, and for IHS it was $2,000 per person.[5] The quality of health care varies widely from reservation to reservation, and cases of neglect and mistreatment are commonly reported, such as the case of "Michael Buckingham, a Makah Indian, [who] lost two fingers in a fishing accident in the waters off his reservation, in the isolated coastal town of Neah Bay,"[6] reported by Vanessa Ho of SeattlePI.com. Ho adds that "Buckingham needed physical therapy for a third finger that was severely injured, but couldn't afford the 70-mile trips to the closest therapy clinic in Port Angeles." Ho also reports that "Elizabeth Buckingham, Michael's mother and the tribe's health director, said the lack of federal funds has caused people to live with chronic pain, pregnant women to forgo prenatal care and many people to suffer from untreated depression. And that's in a place already distraught from drug overdoses and an unemployment rate of 50 percent."

Some conservative commentators use the negative statistics regarding IHS-funded care to argue against government-funded health care. During the highly contentious debates over health care reforms and national health care programs, which ultimately resulted in the passage of the Patient Protection and Affordable Care Act and the Health Care and Education Reconciliation Act of 2010, conservative politicians and commentators pointed to problems within the IHS as a cautionary tale against what was commonly termed "socialized medicine." Senator Tom Coburn of Oklahoma quipped at the conclusion of an article published on FoxNews.com that "single payer, government-run health care has long been a dream of the principal authors of the health 'reform' bills moving through Congress. Any public option, however watered-down, that makes it into [the] final bill will be designed to move us closer to that goal. The American people have good reason to be concerned. If you like Indian Health Services you'll love the public option."[7] Other commentators express hope that the national debate over health care reform will ultimately benefit Native Americans by focusing attention on the issues they face and by increasing funding for the IHS.

Such commentators took issue with conservatives using the IHS as an example of the failures of government-funded health care. Responding to an episode of Fox News' *The Glenn Beck Program*, in which conservative host Beck's guests—government officials and members of several tribes—relayed horror stories of neglect and mistreatment under the IHS, blogger Writing Raven declared, "But who are the people that are throwing road blocks in the way of funding the IHS in the first place? How is it that, despite 'everyone' knowing how terribly underfunded the system is, politicians haven't been able to get any money to it? Was Glenn Beck speaking out against [President George W.] Bush when he was threatening to veto the (as yet made law) Indian Health Care Improvement Act last year [2008]? You can't be a part of the problem, and then use the problem as an example of what the other guy is doing wrong."8

The issues of poverty and lack of access to proper health care are among many of the social and economic concerns facing Native Americans that are examined in *Opposing Viewpoints: Native Americans*. The viewpoints in the book explore major cultural, social, economic, and legal concerns of Native Americans in the following chapters: What Impact Does Discrimination Have on Native American Culture?, What Are Some Key Conflicts Between the US and Tribal Governments?, How Do Disputes over Resources and Artifacts Affect Native Americans?, and What Economic Factors Most Concern Native Americans? The information provided in this volume offers insight into some of the recent controversies surrounding issues such as the use of Native American names and images, legal rights to religious expression, tribal sovereignty, tribal court and criminal justice systems, the protection and repatriation of Native American human remains and artifacts, the use and ownership of natural resources on tribal lands, and the benefits and challenges presented by tribal-owned casinos.

Notes

1. Mary Clare Jalonick, "Promises, Promises: Indian Health Care Needs Unmet," *Seattle Times*, June 15, 2009.
2. *Novo Nordisk Bluesheet*, Issue 4, November 2010, p. 3.
3. Indian Health Service website, Fact Sheet, June 2008. www.ihs.gov.
4. *Novo Nordisk Bluesheet*, Issue 4, November 2010, p. 4.
5. Indian Health Service website, "2005 IHS Expenditures per Capita Compared to Other Federal Health Expenditure Benchmarks," January 2006. http://www.ihs.gov.
6. Vanessa Ho, "Native American Death Rates Soar as Most People Are Living Longer," SeattlePI.com, March 11, 2009. www.seattlepi.com.
7. Senator Tom Coburn, "Don't Get Sick After June," Fox News.com, November 5, 2009. www.foxnews.com.
8. Writing Raven, "Healthcare Video Debate Going for Indian Health Services Tactics," *Alaska Real*, August 24, 2009. http://alaskareal.blogspot.com.

 **OPPOSING VIEWPOINTS® SERIES**

What Impact Does Discrimination Have on Native American Culture?

Chapter Preface

The history of racism against Native Americans is well documented and taught in schools and universities: Native Americans were viewed as "savages" by early European settlers in North America; they were systematically destroyed by smallpox; and they were attacked, their land was taken from them, those who survived were sent to live on reservations, and their children were sent to Indian Schools, where they were instructed to reject their heritage, embrace Christianity, and assimilate into white society. Rather than being a part of long-ago history, however, some commentators insist that this racism continues today and express frustration and anger that it is not more widely recognized or addressed while charges of racism against other groups are swiftly and publicly addressed and denounced. Tim Giago, in an article in the *Huffington Post*, declares that "there is racism against Native Americans in much of America and like the racism against African Americans it needs to be dragged out from under the rug and addressed."[1] Giago's sentiments are echoed by many others who assert that tolerance for racist commentary, jokes, and imagery that target Native Americans, as well as the continued appropriation of Native American names, terms, and images by sports teams, is demeaning and insulting to Native Americans. David Kimelberg, in another *Huffington Post* article, explains, "Today's use and furtherance of stereotypical Native American imagery and narrative only serves to keep shameful concepts alive, regardless of whether it's the actual intent. What's more, they remind Native Americans, particularly our youth, that others do not deem us worthy of respect and that our people are merely a historical holdover to be represented by comic book imagery."[2] Commentators also speculate about the reasons why only those of Native American descent seem to be speaking out against discrimination and racism against Native Americans, while other targeted groups are defended by the majority of society. Giago suggests: "It is almost as if Indians are property, albeit human property, to be possessed by those who would observe, pity, assist or praise them as figments of a vanishing race. Indians can then be safely relegated to the role of mascots for America's fun and games. They can then be honored for what 'they used to be' not for what they are today in modern America. They become warriors, chiefs, redskins and braves, everything but human beings."

Kimelberg and other commentators expressed outrage over the *New Yorker* editors' selection of the caption "Quick, Get Them a Casino" as the winning entry in a contest to provide a caption for a cartoon depicting a man wearing a cowboy hat crouching behind an arrow-riddled desk and speaking into a telephone. Rhonda LeValdo, vice president of the board of directors of the Native American Journalists Association, stated in a letter she sent to the *New Yorker* editors that "not only is the cartoon a form of racism, but it insinuates the stereotype of Native American Indians that we are still hostile. We can't simply do business with Americans, so we have to resort to violence. Ironically, our people were always at the receiving ends of violence by the American government, through massacres inflicted on our people."[3] *Newspaper Rock* blogger Mary Papenfuss asserted, "*New Yorker* readers are supposedly America's liberal elite. This demonstrates how pervasive Native stereotypes are. Even people who know (or should know) better are okay with Indians shooting arrows. It's like having a white man as president or a marriage between a man and a woman—i.e., something Americans have assumed to be true."[4] LeValdo concluded her letter to the *New Yorker* editors by stating, "The Native American Journalists Association would like to extend a hand to your newsroom and explain what racism is. While your cartoon may have just been a tool to get some laughs, our people, our Native Nations are not here to be your comic relief."

The debate over contemporary racism against Native Americans is explored in detail in this chapter. The viewpoints here discuss such issues as the use of the name "Geronimo" as a code name for Osama bin Laden; the controversy over the use of Native American–themed mascots for sports teams; and the debate over whether Native Americans in schools and prisons should be allowed to wear long hair as an expression of religious and cultural beliefs.

Notes

1. Tim Giago, "Racism Against Native Americans Must Be Addressed," *Huffington Post*, October 4, 2009. www.huffington post.com.
2. David Kimelberg, "The Last Acceptable Racism: Native Americans," *Huffington Post*, February 10, 2011. www.huff ingtonpost.com.
3. Rhonda LeValdo, "*New Yorker* 'Caption Contest Winner,'" *Skycity1's Blog*, September 30, 2010. http://skycity1.word press.com.
4. Mary Papenfuss, "Indians Shoot Arrows in *New Yorker* Cartoon," *Newspaper Rock*, September 20, 2010. http://news paperrock.bluecorncomics.com.

> *"Indian peoples feel their sacrifices have been dishonored by the labeling of our worst enemy as Geronimo and that they themselves have been treated as other than real Americans."*

Using "Geronimo" as a Code Name for Osama bin Laden Is Disrespectful to Native Americans

Karl Jacoby

Karl Jacoby is a history professor at Brown University and the author of Shadows at Dawn: A Borderlands Massacre and the Violence of History. *In the following viewpoint, he maintains that the US military and government betrayed and dishonored Native Americans by giving Osama bin Laden—the mastermind behind the September 11, 2001, terrorist attacks on America— the code name "Geronimo," one of the best-known Native Americans. Jacoby provides background information on Geronimo, his history with the US government and military, and asserts that there is no valid comparison between the famed Apache leader*

Karl Jacoby, "Dishonored," *Los Angeles Times*, May 10, 2011, p. A11. Reproduced by permission of the author.

23

and Osama bin Laden. Jacoby further asserts that Native Americans feel that referring to bin Laden as Geronimo belittles Native Americans' military service and contributions to American history. The author concludes that this incident is evidence of a widespread problem in the United States of Americans' unawareness of Native American history and culture.

As you read, consider the following questions:

1. What were Geronimo's real name and tribal affiliation, according to the author?

2. What ethnic group does Jacoby indicate has the highest per capita enlistment rate in the US military?

3. When does Jacoby say the first Native American rights organization was founded, and by whom?

"Geronimo—ekia." With this coded message, sent on May 1 [2011], a U.S. Navy SEALs commando squad signaled the death of Osama bin Laden, the "enemy killed in action." The mission was pulled off without a hitch, but in the week since then, debate has raged in some circles about the code name.

The administration hasn't explained why the operation targeting bin Laden used the name of one of the nation's best-known Native Americans, saying the selection process of names for such missions is confidential. But the use of Geronimo's name speaks to the powerful, if unexamined, hold that the nation's "Indian wars" continue to have on our popular consciousness.

The History of the United States and Geronimo

Geronimo, whose real name was Guyaale, "the Yawner," was a member of the Chiricahua Apache, a group that ranged across New Mexico, Arizona and northern Mexico from the 1820s to the 1880s. His relations with the U.S. were not always hostile. Indeed, as he later reported in his autobiography, his first encounter with government representatives—a small team marking the U.S.-Mexico border in the 1850s—was cordial. "[W]e made a treaty with them by shaking hands and promising to be brothers," recalled Geronimo. "Then we made our camp near their camp, and they came to trade with us."

But after a misunderstanding led to the U.S. Army's attempt to arrest the Chiricahua leader Cochise in 1861, relations between the Chiricahua Apaches and the government deteriorated. On four separate occasions, Geronimo fled the reservations on which the U.S. government had tried to confine him. The Apache leader and the men, women and children accompanying him successfully eluded the army for long periods, supporting themselves with raids on settlements in Arizona and across the border in Mexico. Geronimo's final surrender in 1886 is generally seen as the end of the "Indian wars," giving Geronimo the distinction of being the last Indian to hold out against the U.S. militarily.

Present-day Native American leaders have rightly objected to the implied comparison between Geronimo and bin Laden. As Jeff Houser, chairman of the Fort Sill Apache Tribe noted in a letter to President Obama, "to equate Geronimo ... with Osama bin Laden, a mass murderer and cowardly terrorist, is painful and offensive to our tribe and to all native Americans." No religious fundamentalist, Geronimo never sought to create an all-encompassing caliphate. Rather, he simply wanted to be left alone.

Indian peoples have long played an odd role in American popular culture, seen at once as primitives who are dangerously savage but also authentic, brave and connected to nature. In U.S. military culture, this view has led to Indians being seen as the embodiment of warrior culture. U.S. paratroopers, after watching the 1939 movie *Geronimo*, (a film advertised at the time as featuring images of "war-maddened

Use of "Geronimo" as a Code Name for Osama bin Laden Provokes Shock and Anger

That the assigned code name of Enemy Number One was "Geronimo," a legendary Apache leader ... is being interpreted as a slap in the face of Native people, a disturbing message that equates an iconic symbol of Native American pride with the most hated evildoer since Adolf Hitler.

Lise Balk King,
"Bin Laden Code-Name 'Geronimo'
Is a Bomb in Indian Country,"
Indian Country Today Media Network, May 3, 2011.
http://indiancountrytodaymedianetwork.com.

savages terrorizing the West"), began shouting the Apache leader's name as they jumped from airplanes to bolster their courage. The military has often used Indian names for its helicopters (Kiowa, Cheyenne, Comanche, Blackhawk and, yes, Apache). And now, there is this latest use of Geronimo.

An Outrageous Denial of Native American Contributions

The appropriation of Indian labels is particularly unseemly given the reality of today's military. Native Americans have one of the highest per capita enlistment rates in the military of any ethnic group. Powwows often begin with the entering of an honor guard, composed of military veterans who carry the U.S. and tribal flags. At the San Carlos Apache Reservation in Arizona, where Geronimo was confined in the 1870s and '80s, the tribal government maintains a billboard proudly listing all the San Carlos Apaches serving in the military.

It's no wonder that Indian peoples feel their sacrifices have been dishonored by the labeling of our worst enemy as Geronimo and that they themselves have been treated as other than real Americans. As Guyaale's great-grandson, Joseph Geronimo, noted recently, using the name in the operation to kill bin Laden was a "slap in the face." His ancestor, after all, "was more American than anybody else."

Widespread Ignorance of Native American History and Culture

But more than its misguided comparison of two individuals, the whole episode reminds us that we do not yet fully grasp our Native American past. If Americans know so little about Geronimo, probably the most famous Indian in American history, how many know anything at all about some of Geronimo's contemporaries, who laid the groundwork for the Indian rights movement? How many have ever heard, say, of Carlos Montezuma, the Yavapai with a medical degree from Northwestern, who in 1911 founded the first Indian rights organization, the Society of American Indians? Or Sarah Winnemucca, who wrote an autobiography about her Paiute heritage and became an early advocate on behalf of Indian peoples?

Beyond reckoning with its Native American past, the U.S. needs to think about its Native American present and future, too. Despite the fabled wealth of a few Native American communities from the recent rise of casino gambling, most of Indian country remains desperately impoverished. The unemployment rate on Geronimo's onetime home of San Carlos, for example, is today close to 70%. Imagine if Operation Geronimo, rather than a mission to seize a terrorist in distant Pakistan, had been instead a U.S. effort to address the endemic poverty that haunts many Indian reservations today. Would that not have represented a long-overdue American victory as well?

> *"I don't see any disrespect in writing the fabled name of Geronimo into American history one more time, as part of a great victory for freedom, and justice for so many murdered families."*

Using "Geronimo" as a Code Name for Osama bin Laden Is Not Disrespectful to Native Americans

John Hayward

John Hayward is a staff writer for Human Events. *In the following viewpoint, he dismisses charges that the US military and government dishonored Native Americans by giving terrorist Osama bin Laden the code name "Geronimo," one of the best-known Native Americans. Hayward describes Geronimo as a fierce warrior and points out that parts of his personal history are unfavorable. The author argues that irrespective of the actual facts of Geronimo's life, including that his real name was not Geronimo, the Apache warrior's legend and legacy have been part of American culture for years in various ways. Hayward*

John Hayward, "Code Geronimo: Was the Choice of Operation Names an Insult?," *Human Events*, May 5, 2011. Reproduced by permission.

contends that Americans, including the American military, honor the warrior spirit and courage of Native Americans by naming weapons systems, sports teams, and military operations after them.

As you read, consider the following questions:

1. How many soldiers were needed to corner Geronimo and his men in the Sonora mountains, according to Hayward?

2. What does Hayward say that the Navy SEALs commandos who killed bin Laden owe to Geronimo and the Apaches?

3. Why does Hayward suggest the code name "Geronimo" was chosen for bin Laden?

There have been some complaints from Native Americans about the use of the code name "Geronimo" during the operation that killed Osama bin Laden. Geronimo's great-grandson Harlyn [Geronimo] is particularly upset. "Whether it was intended only to name the military operation to kill or capture Osama bin Laden or to give Osama bin Laden himself the code name Geronimo, either was an outrageous insult and mistake," he said in a statement. He wants Defense Secretary Robert Gates to explain "how this disgraceful use of my great-grandfather's name occurred," and purge the name from all official records of the assault on bin Laden's compound.

The government responded in several predictable fashions. First they laughably denied that the "Geronimo" code name referred to bin Laden himself. This is obviously not true—the SEAL who spotted bin Laden said "We have a visual on Geronimo," while the code for his successful eradication was "Geronimo-EKIA." It's really splitting hairs to claim the name was not being used as a reference for the primary target of the mission.

Outrage over Code Name "Geronimo" Is Part of Religious Left Mythology

History can decide whether naming the bin Laden operation [referring to the US military's mission to capture terrorist leader Osama bin Laden] after Geronimo was wise or even consequential. What is more noteworthy are the endless exertions of some Western church elites to avoid confronting bin Laden's brand of evil while constructing endless fantasies to demonize America.

Mark Tooley, "Geronimo and Osama,"
American Spectator, *May 13, 2011.*

Next, our ponderous federal bureaucracy began using its flabby arms to spank itself, as the Senate Committee on Indian Affairs "took the opportunity to discuss complaints by some Native Americans" about the Geronimo code name. There was some anguish over "inappropriate uses of Native American icons and cultures" which are "prevalent through our society."

People feel what they feel. If Harlyn Geronimo takes the use of his ancestor's name as an insult, no one can tell him he's "wrong," although we may fairly mourn the increasing amount of mourning in our high-strung society. I would ask him to reconsider, though.

The Real History of Geronimo

"Geronimo" is not actually the great Apache warrior's name. His real name is rendered as "Goyathlay," "Goyaale," or "Goyahkla" in various sources. "Geronimo" was a nickname—a code name, if you will—said to have been given to him by the Mexicans, who probably called him a great many things during his years of war against them. He was later written into history by Americans who never heard any other name for him.

He was a husband and father before he became a warrior. Mexican soldiers killed his family, and he ran through hails of gunfire with a knife in his hand to avenge them. He fought white settlers too, with a ferocity that intensified after the government tried to force his Chiricahua Apache tribe onto a bleak reservation in Arizona.

The difficulty of catching Geronimo was a matter of legend. It took five thousand soldiers half a year to corner his band of a hundred raiders in the Sonora mountains . . . and a few days after surrendering, he changed his mind. Another six months passed before the government lured him into another surrender, offering a promise of temporary exile in Florida. Like all temporary government programs, his exile from Arizona ended up lasting forever.

Some of the things Geronimo did were terrible. His courage and determination were glorious. It would truly dishonor his memory to forget either of those truths. He was so famous that he marched in President Theodore Roosevelt's inaugural parade in 1905. He was so lonely that he died of pneumonia after being thrown from his horse four years later, and spending a night lying in the rain.

Legend and Legacy Are Subjective

His legend is part of America's legend now. Would the most unforgettable of Apaches have approved? Would those who died in battle against him? It doesn't matter, because history is not an act of consensus. The future will remember what it remembers, just as people feel what they feel.

Osama bin Laden is a part of our history too, and few among us are pleased about it. (I will not say "none," because that would not be true.) He was tough to catch. The men who took him down made a bold leap into dangerous territory to get the job done. Their commando training owes much to what Geronimo and the Apaches added to the American understanding of warfare.

There's an old cliché about people shouting "Geronimo!" when they jump out of airplanes, but Geronimo wasn't a paratrooper. They use his name because they remember his bravery, a century after the passing of the last people who would have used his name as a curse.

The Military Honors Geronimo's Spirit

It's inconceivable that anyone connected with Operation Geronimo intended the name as an insult to the Apache or his descendants. To assume otherwise comically underestimates the eagerness of official America to avoid offending segments of our population that have their own Senate committees. We may never know for sure, but I suspect the name was chosen because it's so familiar. If there was any deeper significance, it may lie in the courageous way our SEALs ended a very long hunt.

No one in their right minds thinks the sniveling coward who answered for over three thousand murders last Sunday [in May 2011] has anything in common with the eternal avatar of the Apache warrior spirit. The U.S. military doesn't name its weapon systems after "Native American icons and cultures" as a gesture of *contempt*. Sports teams are not given Indian names because the fans look down on Indians. His great-grandson may choose to disagree, but I don't see any disrespect in writing the fabled name of Geronimo into American history one more time, as part of a great victory for freedom, and justice for so many murdered families.

> "The negative environment perpetuated by Indian mascots undermines our cultures, our traditions, and our spirituality."

Native American–Themed Sports Mascots Are Racist and Reinforce Negative Stereotypes

Tex G. Hall

Tex G. Hall served two terms as president of the National Congress of American Indians and is the chairman of the Mandan, Hidatsa, and Arikara Nation in North Dakota. He has worked as school principal and superintendent. In the following viewpoint Hall, on behalf of the Mandan, Hidatsa, and Arikara Nation, declares his opposition to the use of Native American images as mascots by sports teams. He explains in detail the Standing Rock Sioux tribe's case against the University of North Dakota's use of the Fighting Sioux mascot, and he expresses his support for that tribe's position. Hall declares that the use of such images is racist and demeaning; especially when their use is

Tex G. Hall, "Testimony of Hon. Tex G. Hall, Chairman of the Mandan, Hidatsa and Arikara Nation, Chairman of the Great Plains Tribal Chairman's Association, On Mascots, Stereotypes, and Native Americans," US Senate Committee on Indian Affairs, May 5, 2011.

sanctioned by educational institutions, they create a negative and inaccurate portrayal of Native Americans that hurts young Native Americans' educational prospects and damages their self-esteem.

As you read, consider the following questions:

1. According to Hall, what were the terms of the University of North Dakota's agreement with the NCAA regarding its use of the "Fighting Sioux" nickname and logo?

2. What professional baseball team's logo does Hall characterize as "grossly demeaning"?

3. What organizations does Hall cite as being against the use of Native American–themed mascots, nicknames, and logos?

I am testifying today on behalf of the Mandan, Hidatsa, and Arika Nation and the Great Plains Tribal Chairman's Association.

I wish to thank the Committee [US Senate Committee on Indian Affairs] and the Chairman for bringing this important topic into the public spotlight. As you know, where I am from, this is quite the controversial issue. The University of North Dakota's [UND's] continued use of the name and image of the "Fighting Sioux" has landed us in the middle of a national media firestorm.

Too often though, the debate rages all around us, while we, the First Americans, often have the last word. I hope that this hearing will bring our voice to the forefront of the debate and provide some clarity and guidance for schools and people across the country.

As you know, there are many who view the use of Native American images by colleges or universities to be heroic, spirited, or just generally positive. On the other hand, there are many others who argue that the use of such images promotes negative stereotypes, which can be offensive, demeaning and insensitive.

While I cannot speak for every single Native American in this country, I can speak from my experiences as a school-teacher, sports team player, coach, and tournament administrator, as well as the elected leader of my tribe and a representative of many more.

My position, and the position of my tribe, and many others is this—we find the use of Native American mascots to be dehumanizing and disrespectful. I have submitted a resolution passed last month [April 2011] by the Great Plains Tribal Chairman's Association supporting the NCAA's [National Collegiate Athletic Association's] efforts to eliminate the use of American Indian mascots, and supporting the University of North Dakota's Senate, the university's Student Senate, the North Dakota State Board of Higher Education and the North Dakota Senate Education Committee's call to stop the university from using the "Fighting Sioux" nickname and logo.

University of North Dakota Fighting Sioux Controversy

As you know, the University of North Dakota reached an agreement with the NCAA in 2007 to stop using the nickname and logo by August 15, 2011, unless it received approval from two of North Dakota's tribes—the Spirit Lake and Standing Rock Sioux tribes. The Standing Rock Sioux tribe has been firmly opposed to the use of the "Fighting Sioux" and thus the university, if it is to comply with its own promise, must stop using the name and logo this year.

This situation has been complicated by a law passed this year by the North Dakota legislature, and signed by the governor, requiring the university to keep the "Fighting Sioux" name and logo. The law has also raised the issue of whether the North Dakota attorney general will sue the NCAA.

"But I'm honoring you, Dude," cartoon by Lalo Alcaraz. Copyright © 2002 Lalo Alcaraz. Used by permission of Universal Uclick. All rights reserved.

The NCAA just reminded the university that nothing has changed since 2007 and that the settlement agreement still stands. And, since the Standing Rock Sioux tribe has not authorized the university to keep the Fighting Sioux mascot, then the university has to no choice but to abide by the terms that it agreed to and retire the Fighting Sioux mascot. Otherwise, the NCAA could impose sanctions including barring UND teams from hosting postseason tournaments or wearing proscribed attire during those tournaments. The NCAA also said that in its view, the North Dakota law "cannot change the NCAA policy nor alter the contracted terms of the agreement."

As I testified earlier, our tribe and the Great Plains Tribal Chairman's Association stand with the Standing Rock Sioux tribe on this issue and call on the university to start shopping for a new mascot and logo.

Concerns for the Next Generation

My tribe's concerns arise out of our concern for our children. We believe that every child has the potential to be a great leader, athlete, scholar, president, or medicine man or woman. We try and teach them that nothing can hold them back. But at the same time, we recognize that there are forces built on institutional racism and economic reality that can sometimes hold them back. My administration is built on hope and opportunity, and one thing that we can do something about is challenging negative cultural stereotypes.

The sad reality is that most mascot names that refer to Native Americans reinforce negative cultural stereotypes: [the Washington] Redskins, the Fighting Sioux, and the grossly demeaning Cleveland Indians logo. We want to make sure that all of our children have the opportunity to create his or her own image for themselves and not have images created for them, whether by the universities, high schools, or the media.

The American Psychological Association summed up this issue by stating:

> "The use of American Indian mascots as symbols in schools and university athletic programs is particularly troubling because schools are places of learning. These mascots are teaching stereotypical, misleading, and, too often, insulting images of American Indians. These negative lessons are not just affecting American Indian students; they are sending the wrong message to all students."
>
> —*Former APA President Ronald F. Levant*

We believe that the use of Indian mascots create a negative environment for our Native American students, and other students too, by creating a hostile learning environment, by reaffirming negative stereotypes of American Indians that most of us grew up with, and by grossly misinforming students (and adults) who have had no or little contact with Native Americans in the first place. The negative environment perpetuated by Indian mascots undermines our cultures, our traditions, and our spirituality. And, as with most forms of institutional racism, the use of those images are perpetuated by institutions which have power.

And that is why I am glad to be here to speak to these powers. And that is why I am glad to have your support and friendship, Mr. Chairman, and committee members. Together, we can fight power with power.

To this end, I would like to remind the committee that we do not stand alone. The National Congress of American Indians, the National Education Association, the American Psychological Association, and the NCAA stand with us.

An Opportunity to Remove Barriers

NBA [National Basketball Association] legend and University of North Dakota graduate Phil Jackson asked the university not too long ago, "What is to be gained by keeping the Fighting Sioux?" The "objectification of people is limiting to ourselves" as well as to the people we objectify. "We have a chance to do the right thing."

We have a chance to make a change for the better, to make our children's lives richer and to lift the bonds of oppression surrounding them.

I hope that the University of North Dakota, and all schools, do indeed take the chance and do the right thing.

"*I would like the general public to know why redskin is a detrimental term. But as far as the Warriors, Braves and Indians—that to me is a source of pride.*"

Most Native American–Themed Sports Mascots Are Flattering and Not Racist

Rain Smith

Rain Smith is a contributing reporter to Timesnews.net and various affiliated newspaper publications. In the following viewpoint, Smith disputes the notion that all Native Americans believe that all Native American–themed mascots are racist and declares that most Native Americans are in favor of such mascots. Smith cites Native Americans and poll numbers to illustrate that there are many Native Americans who believe that when schools and sports teams use Native American imagery and names such as Braves, Warriors, or Indians for their mascots, they are honoring the strength and courage of Native Americans.

Rain Smith, "Local Native American Leader Opposes Banning All Indian Mascots from School: 'I Personally Think It's an Honor,'" Timesnews.net, January 24, 2007. Reproduced by permission.

One mascot name, however, that Smith presents as offensive to most Native Americans is "redskins," which the author explains has violent and racist origins.

As you read, consider the following questions:

1. According to the *Sports Illustrated* poll cited in the viewpoint, what percentage of Native Americans do not think that schools and colleges should refrain from using Native American–themed nicknames?

2. What team name does athletic director Cary Daniels say symbolizes strength and courage without being disrespectful to Native Americans?

3. According to Chief Lee Vest, how did the term "redskins" originate, and to what does it refer?

As activists prepare to request state officials ban the use of Indian mascots in public schools, a local American Indian leader says the use of Indians, Warriors and Braves is actually an honor.

"[There're] more important things—as far as health care and education—so that's not a priority to me," said Chief Lee Vest of the Appalachian Confederated Tribes, an organization of more than 300 American Indian descendants throughout the region. "I personally think it's an honor to be chosen (as a mascot)."

Close to two dozen Tennessee high schools—including Kingsport's Dobyns-Bennett [D-B] and Rogersville's Cherokee—and 80 middle and elementary schools—such as John Sevier, Robison and Indian Springs—use American Indian mascots. This has prompted members of the Tennessee Commission of Indian Affairs to go before the state's Human Right's Commission on Friday [in January 2007], declare the mascots offensive and request they be banned in state public schools.

The National Congress of American Indians says debate over Indian sports mascots dates back to the 1970s, when the University of Oklahoma changed its mascot, Little Red. In 2005 the NCAA [National Collegiate Athletic Association] banned the use of Indian mascots in postseason tournaments.

Most Native Americans Support Mascots

Though Vest's Appalachian Confederated Tribes is part of the Tennessee Commission of Indian Affairs, he says his group is not in support of an all-encompassing ban on Indian mascots.

"When I was in high school (outside Roanoke, Va.) I was a Proud Warrior—the Warrior was our mascot," Vest said. "I played football and ran track and personally loved (the team mascot). I remember being in football games with that Warrior Spirit, and here we were as the Warriors. It actually got my juices flowing, so to speak."

According to a poll conducted by *Sports Illustrated* in 2002, the majority of American Indians agree with Vest. The poll found 81% of American Indian respondents do not think high school and college teams should stop using Indian nicknames. As for professional athletics, 83% of Native American respondents said teams should not stop using Indian nicknames, mascots, characters and symbols.

Reaction to the Commission of Indian Affairs' request for a ban has riled supporters of the Dobyns-Bennett High School Indians. Lib Dudney, a former D-B teacher and current president of the school's education foundation, says the mascot honors the region's heritage, and "you don't name a mascot after something you want to put down."

"We're not putting them down, we're honoring them," Dudney said. "As a D-B student, teacher and alumnus, that's how I've always felt about it, and everyone I know feels that way."

D-B Athletic Director Cary Daniels believes athletic teams want strong, courageous symbols that can be admired as a mascot. The title of "Indians," he says, fits that role while paying no disrespect.

Principal of John Sevier Middle School, Carolyn McPherson, applied the same logic to her school's mascot, the Warriors, saying it denotes courage and positive attributes.

"Warriors is a source of pride for us, something we're very proud of," she said.

Redskins Is a Highly Offensive Term

And while in agreement that Indians and Warriors are not disparaging terms, Vest does note one mascot as offensive—compares it to racial slurs against African Americans.

"Even though people say they're silly for protesting it, the biggest problem for all Native Americans is the use of Redskin," Vest said.

Both Robison Middle School in Kingsport and Indian Springs Elementary—where Vest's own children attended and he continues to provide educational programs for students—are nicknamed the Redskins. Activists across the nation have long protested the use of Redskins for Washington's NFL [National Football League] franchise, even as the Smithsonian Institution's senior linguist argues American Indians first used the word in the 18th century.

For the majority of American Indians, the hypothesis their people coined redskin to distinguish themselves from "others" encroaching on their lands doesn't mask racist connotations.

Researchers' theories also fail to explain how the word—no matter who created it—was assimilated into our nation's vernacular.

"They were paid money for killing women and children—not just men," Vest said of bounties put on heads of "savage" American Indians. "The scalp was the proof they were killed, and it was not thought of as inhumane.

"Then some unscrupulous white people would see a Caucasian with dark hair and started killing Caucasians for bounty money, so something needed to be done. They came up with, 'bring us some redskin.' To get the bounty they then not only had to bring the scalp in, but the genitals of a man. They'd do the same to a woman, either her breast or her genitals—and those were called 'redskins.'"

If history textbooks would mention such gory details of genocide, Vest believes the general public would understand why "redskin" is an offensive term.

"If the Indian community hates these names, the Indian community needs to explain why," Vest said. "I would like the general public to know why redskin is a detrimental term. But as far as the Warriors, Braves and Indians—that to me is a source of pride."

Periodical and Internet Sources Bibliography

The following articles have been selected to supplement the diverse views presented in this chapter.

American Civil Liberties Union	"Native American Student Suspended for Refusal to Cut Hair," March 18, 2011. http://www.aclu.org.
Associated Press	"In Wake of Geronimo Controversy, Senate Indian Panel to Discuss Racial Concerns," *Corpus Christi Caller-Times*, May 5, 2011.
Paula Boivin	"Native Community Divided on Mascots," *Arizona Republic*, February 1, 2008.
Cindy Brovsky	"Legislators Fume over Native American Mascots," *Colorado Statesman*, January 29, 2010.
Monica Davey	"Insult or Honor?," *New York Times Upfront*, vol. 142, February 8, 2010.
Ernestine Chasing Hawk	"Code Name: Geronimo?," *Native Sun News*, May 4, 2011.
Paul Knight	"A Native American Family Fights Against Hair Length Rules," *Houston Press*, July 9, 2008.
Steven T. Newcomb	"Geronimo Again? The Indian Wars Continue *Ad Nauseam*," Indian Country Today Media Network, May 3, 2011. http://indiancountry todaymedianetwork.com.
Victoria Rossi	"Justin-Siena Works with Wappo Tribe to Create 'Braves' Mascot," *Napa Valley Register*, April 9, 2011.
Neely Tucker	"American Indians Object to 'Geronimo' as Code for Bin Laden Raid," *Washington Post*, May 3, 2011.

OPPOSING
VIEWPOINTS®
SERIES

CHAPTER 2

What Are Some Key Conflicts Between the US and Tribal Governments?

Chapter Preface

Experts have identified an alarming trend in rising numbers of reported incidents of domestic violence on Native American reservations that some have characterized as a full-blown crisis in such communities. The ongoing debate over root causes and most appropriate means of addressing this issue illustrates the inherent difficulties presented by tribal sovereignty, which is the principle that underlies the complex relationship between the US government that provides resources and funding for aid and services for Native Americans, and the tribal governments that determine how to best make use of those resources and funding to address the needs of their constituents. An Amnesty International report from 2007[1] explains that not only are Native American women victims of domestic violence at rates that are more than two and a half times the national average, but in 86 percent of cases, they are victimized by non–Native American men, according to a US Department of Justice report.[2] The latter fact complicates both the reporting of the crime and the prosecution of the abuser, as tribal criminal justice systems have neither the authority nor the resources necessary to pursue, apprehend, and prosecute outside of their jurisdictions. Further complicating matters is the confusing maze of tribal, state, and federal laws that govern Native American reservations, and the reluctance of Native American community members to seek help from a law enforcement system that they view as abusive and excessively punitive and that conflicts dramatically with Native Americans' beliefs in restorative justice. "Barriers to reporting include fear of breaches in confidentiality, fear of retaliation and a lack of confidence that reports will be taken seriously and result in perpetrators being brought to justice. For Native American and Alaska Native women, historical relations with federal and state government agencies also affect the level of reporting of sexual violence," according to the Amnesty International report.

The US Department of Justice has reported that national statistics show that one in five women will be sexually assaulted during their lifetimes, while the rate among Native American women is more than one in three.[3] Amnesty International's report indicates that these figures do not even represent the entirety of the problem of domestic violence among Native American women, because many incidents are never reported. "Most women who are beaten or raped don't report to the police. They just shower and go to the clinic [for treatment]," according to a Native American survivor of sexual violence quoted in the Amnesty International report. Matthew L.M. Fletcher, a law professor at Michigan State University, declares that "unprosecuted domestic violence committed by non-Indians in Indian Country is a serious problem, without an effective federal or state solution absent an Act of Congress. The Supreme Court has created—and Congress has not done enough to solve—a terrible irony. The law enforcement jurisdiction closest to the crime and with the greatest capacity and motivation for responding quickly, efficiently, and fairly, has been stripped of the authority to react, leaving Indian women to suffer, and crimes of domestic violence to remain unresolved and unprosecuted."[4] The Tribal Law and Order Act, which was signed into law in 2010, is an attempt to address some of the challenges facing tribal criminal justice systems and to assist them in improving relations with and support of Native American communities by granting broader authority to law enforcement and courts, providing better training for public safety officers, and fostering better communication between government agencies and tribal authorities, among other measures. While some Native American and women's advocacy groups object to the Tribal Law and Order Act for what they characterize as an overemphasis on punishment rather than on education and rehabilitation, other groups have praised it as a significant step toward reducing the incidence of violence against Native American women.

Debate over how to address high domestic violence rates on reservations is only one of many conflicts between the US and tribal governments. The viewpoints in this chapter address the debate over the US government's role in and attempts to address the problems faced by tribal court systems; what should be done to solve issues within the Bureau of Indian Affairs; and the relative merits and effectiveness of the Tribal Law and Order Act.

Notes

1. Amnesty International, *Maze of Injustice: The Failure to Protect Indigenous Women from Sexual Violence in the USA*, Amnesty International Publications, 2007.
2. Patricia Tjaden and Nancy Thoennes, *Full Report of the Prevalence, Incidence, and Consequences of Violence Against Women*, US Department of Justice, 2000.
3. Steven W. Perry, *American Indians and Crime—A BJS Statistical Profile 1992–2002*, Bureau of Justice Statistics, US Department of Justice, December 2004.
4. Matthew L.M. Fletcher, "Addressing the Epidemic of Domestic Violence in Indian Country by Restoring Tribal Sovereignty," American Constitution Society for Law and Policy, March 2009.

| "The federal government has fallen far short in addressing the critical public safety problems in Indian Country."

The US Government Has Failed to Adequately Support Tribal Courts

Theresa M. Pouley

Theresa M. Pouley is chief judge of the Tulalip Tribal Court in Tulalip, Washington, and president of the Northwest Tribal Court Judges Association. In the following viewpoint, Pouley demonstrates how the lack of adequate funding and support from the US government greatly hinders the Tulalip Tribal Court's ability to prosecute crimes committed in its jurisdiction and has a tremendously negative impact on the safety and well-being of Native Americans. The author discusses the history of the tribal court and criminal justice systems, describing how the Tulalip Tribes took on responsibility for funding and administering them in the absence and failure of federal and state government support. Pouley cites federal statistics indicating extremely high rates of violent crimes committed on tribal lands and argues that the

Theresa M. Pouley, "Statement of Honorable Theresa M. Pouley, Judge, Tulalip Tribal Court President, Northwest Tribal Court Judges Association," US Senate Committee on Indian Affairs, July 24, 2008.

advantages and demonstrated successes of tribal court systems cannot be sustained without further support from the federal government.

As you read, consider the following questions:

1. According to the viewpoint, what was the annual dollar amount of funding promised for tribal court systems under the Indian Tribal Justice Support Act?

2. According to the Department of Justice–Bureau of Justice Statistics report cited in the viewpoint, what percentage of Native American women will be raped in their lifetime?

3. Why are the Tulalip Tribes' sources of income insufficient to support its public safety infrastructure?

A quality justice system is a central component of the right of a people to make their own laws and be ruled by them. Congress has expressly recognized the importance of tribal courts in enacting the Indian Tribal Justice Act "to assist in the development of tribal justice systems." In enacting this law, Congress recognized that "tribal justice systems are an essential part of tribal governments and serve as important forums for ensuring public health and safety and the political integrity of tribal governments."

The findings of Congress, however, are often at odds with the actions, or inaction, of federal agencies vested with a trust obligation to provide public safety in Indian Country. While the Indian Tribal Justice Support Act promised $58 million for tribal court systems per year, tribal courts have yet to see any funding under this Act. The vast majority of tribes continue to struggle to meet basic public safety needs based on lack of federal support. The [Indian Tribal Justice Act] did result in the creation of the 2000 report of tribal justice systems prepared for the Bureau of Indian Affairs. The report confirmed the competency of tribal courts, found that tribal justice systems are severely under-funded, and recommended base funding levels for tribal courts. Although the federal government has fallen far short in addressing the critical public safety problems in Indian Country, Tulalip and other Indian tribes fortunate enough in recent years to raise revenues through gaming and new business enterprises have started taking on the primary role of law enforcement on the Reservation. Since taking on this responsibility, Tulalip and other Northwest tribes have seen crime rates begin to drop, and the quality of life on the Reservation improve. Taking a lead role in criminal justice has gone hand in hand with steady gains in economic development and employment opportunities on the Reservation. Tulalip recognizes, however, that these gains are fragile, without reliable funding sources that traditionally fund government justice systems.

The Tulalip tribes, NICS [Northwest Intertribal Court System] and the Northwest Tribal Court Judges [Association] support provisions in the proposed Tribal Law and Order Act of 2008 which seek to hold the federal government more accountable for addressing the serious crime problems in Indian Country. The tribes believe that the federal government must do a better job of supporting and empowering tribal justice systems. Toward this end, we strongly support the extension of criminal sentencing authority as necessary in certain cases to protect the Reservation community from dangerous offenders.

I encourage the Committee [US Senate Committee on Indian Affairs] to identify further measures to support and fund strong tribal law enforcement and court operations. More direct funding to tribal courts is drastically needed. The Tulalip Tribes wholeheartedly supports the additional authorization of tribal justice system funding. . . . In addition to federal funding, Congress has a role to play in authorizing an expansion of tribal government taxing authority to raise revenues for tribal justice systems—justice systems that benefit both Indians and non-Indians who reside in and around Reservation communities. . . .

The History of the Tulalip Justice System

The Tulalip Tribes is organized under a Constitution and by-laws adopted by the Tribes and approved by the Secretary of Interior in 1936 pursuant to the Indian Reorganization Act [IRA]. The Tribe is governed by a seven-member board of directors, who are elected to three-year terms. The Tulalip Constitution provides authority for establishment of a tribal judiciary, empowering the Tribes governing body to provide for the maintenance of law and order and the administration of justice by establishing a court system. Despite the federal government's stated commitment under the Indian Reorganization Act to foster tribal self-determination, the goals of the policy went largely unfulfilled due to lack of federal support and little economic opportunity for tribal members residing on the Reservation. In the years following the IRA, there were simply no funds to carry out the basic functions of tribal self-government.

State Assumption of Criminal Jurisdiction Is Not the Solution

In order to address the problems associated with inadequate federal criminal justice resources, the Tulalip Tribes requested the State of Washington in 1958 to assume criminal jurisdiction. . . . However, Tulalip soon found out that State assumption of criminal jurisdiction was not an effective remedy for the public safety problem. The county failed to dedicate adequate police resources to the Reservation, in part because the county received no tax revenues from tribal trust lands. As a result, little improvement was made in crime rates or public safety on the Reservation.

During this period of the 1950s through the mid-1990s, Tulalip was failing to provide the most basic of services to its community—police and criminal justice. The Reservation remained a difficult place to live, and job opportunities were limited. Law enforcement and criminal justice on the Reservation was at best inadequate, and at worst nonexistent. Older tribal members often speak of the harsh conditions on the Reservation during most of this time, when serious crimes such as murder, rape and aggravated assaults often went uninvestigated and perpetrators were not prosecuted or punished.

Building an Effective Tribal Justice System at Tulalip

The Tulalip tribal justice system has made great strides in the last decade. Tribal law enforcement has gone from a single part-time officer to a full-service police department of 47 officers and staff protecting the community seven days a week. The Tribal Court has evolved from part-time operations in an old trailer to a large modular facility with two full-service courtrooms and a complement of court staff operating five days a week. Crime rates have dropped and the quality of life in the community is improving. The Tulalip Tribes has taken on this responsibility to build its own criminal justice system on the Reservation largely because the federal government has failed to fulfill its responsibility, and the state criminal authority proved ineffective.

The Tribes recent success in criminal justice is attributable to two key factors: (1) retrocession of state criminal jurisdiction ..., and (2) new tribal economic development on the Reservation generating much-needed revenues and creating new jobs.

Tulalip Tribes Assume Primary Law Enforcement Responsibilities

The Tulalip Tribes has gradually increased its law enforcement and tribal justice system budget to more than five million dollars annually. These increases have come almost entirely from tribal sources, with the federal government's share of the total budget declining.

Inadequate Funding
for Tribal Courts

Tribal courts agonize over the very same issues that state and federal courts confront in a criminal context, such as assault and battery, child sexual abuse, alcohol and substance abuse, gang violence, violence against women, and now methamphetamines, along with the social ills that are left in its wake.

If tribal courts were not functioning, the respective federal and state court systems would be overwhelmed with the caseload, which we unofficially estimate at around 1.6 million cases per year, which I am sure the federal and state courts would not want, especially given the traditional and customary laws that lay the foundation for tribal statutory and common laws. . . .

On average, small tribal judicial systems handle 250 to 1,500 cases per year, whereas medium to large tribal justice systems handle over 1,500 to 20,000 cases per year. With a disproportionate funding of tribal justice systems, a medium to large justice system may have one judge handling a caseload of up to 5,000 cases a year at a median salary of $40,000 per year.

The fallacy contained herein is that the federal and state courts are adequately funded, yet scrutinize the ability of tribal court judges in their decision making. However, tribal court judges maintain excellence in applying tradition and customs in their respective courts, while being underfunded.

Roman J. Duran,
"Statement of Honorable Roman J. Duran, First Vice President,
National American Indian Court Judges Association,"
US Senate Committee on Indian Affairs, July 24, 2008.

This tribal investment in criminal justice is starting to pay off. Tulalip criminal statistics demonstrate improvements in law enforcement and the justice system are starting to lower crime rates.

The criminal statistics show a steady decline in crime from 2003 through 2007. In 2007, the number of infractions has almost doubled, from 140 in 2006 to 260 in 2007. Thus, excluding traffic, criminal cases declined about 12%. . . .

The Federal Role in Indian Country Justice

Despite the recent gains by Tulalip and other tribes in fighting crime, Indian tribes cannot solve the public safety problem on their own. Due to jurisdictional constraints, and lack of traditional funding sources, tribes must rely on the federal government to play an important role in addressing Reservation crime problems. Tribes rely on the federal government for prosecution of most, but not all, major crimes. Tribes must also rely on federal and/or state prosecution of non-Indian criminal offenders on the Reservation.

Indian Country continues to face a crisis of violent crime. A Bureau of Justice Statistics report covering the period 1992–2002 found that American Indians are victims of violent crime at a rate more than twice that of the national population. According the DOJ-BJS [US Department of Justice–Bureau of Justice Statistics] report, American Indians experienced an estimated one violent crime for every 10 residents over age 12. The figures are even worse for Native American women, who are the victims of rape or sexual assault at a rate more than 2.5 times that of American women in general. The DOJ-BJS study concluded that 34.1 percent of American Indian and Alaska Native women—more than one in three—will be raped in their lifetime. This level of violence against native women is tragic and unacceptable. The majority of perpetrators of violent crime against Indians were non-Indian. Because tribes have been stripped of jurisdiction over non-Indian offenders, tribes need the assistance of federal law enforcement. The Department of Justice must work cooperatively with tribal law enforcement and dramatically step up its efforts to combat this crisis. . . .

Because tribal justice systems are the most effective means of addressing the public safety problems on Reservations, federal funds used to support tribal justice systems are funds well spent. Tulalip has demonstrated that if sufficient resources are dedicated to tribal justice systems, real gains can be made in addressing the serious public safety problems in Indian Country. We urge the Committee to authorize increased federal funding to what works best—building quality tribal justice systems. . . .

The Need for Greater Federal Support and Funding for Tribal Courts

The experience at Tulalip has demonstrated that, given adequate resources, tribal courts provide the most effective means of addressing the problem of crime in reservation communities. Tulalip has seen firsthand the dramatic change in serious criminal behavior from a crisis situation a couple of decades ago to one in which crimes are being steadily reduced. The difference has been the result of a comprehensive tribal police presence on the Reservation accompanied by an effective tribal court justice system.

Tulalip has been able to step forward and make a difference due to recent gains in economic development brought about by its gaming and business enterprises. However, these business revenues are subject to economic cycles and other factors outside the Tulalip Tribes control. A business downturn could easily put the Tribes public safety gains at risk. Like all tribal governments, Tulalip's public safety infrastructure needs a reliable source of government revenue.

The Tulalip Tribes urges this committee to enhance the tribal Law and Order Act by not only authorizing an increase in sentencing authority, but by authorizing an increase in tribal justice system funding. No other governmental entity has a greater stake in reducing reservation crime than the tribal governments themselves. What tribal courts need to be successful is sufficient levels of reliable support—in terms of training, technical assistance, and funding. . . . An increase in direct tribal funding should be complemented by legislation that empowers tribal government to raise revenues themselves to meet their public safety needs. Recent Supreme Court cases which limit taxation powers of tribal governments create serious obstacles for tribes struggling to fund public safety needs. Taxation provides a steady and reliable source of revenue that is now effectively foreclosed to tribal governments due to land status and de facto [established but not necessarily legally ordained] limits on taxation of persons and businesses operating in Indian Country.

> *"Various federal efforts exist that could help to address some of the challenges that tribes face in effectively adjudicating crime in Indian country."*

The US Government Has Greatly Improved Its Support for Tribal Courts

United States Government Accountability Office

The United States Government Accountability Office (GAO) is the investigative agency for the US Congress that studies matters that concern public funds when requested by members of Congress. In the following viewpoint, the GAO reports on the ongoing efforts within various federal agencies to support and augment tribal court systems nationwide. The report acknowledges the numerous challenges faced by tribal courts and law enforcement and notes the disproportionate rate of crime on Indian reservations. The GAO outlines the ways in which the federal government is helping to strengthen tribal court and law enforcement powers to better equip them to handle the challenges they face and remarks on how various improvements in the communica-

Indian Country Criminal Justice: Departments of the Interior and Justice Should Strengthen Coordination to Support Tribal Courts, United States Government Accountability Office: Homeland Security and Justice, February 2011, pp. 1–5, 24–27, 34–36.

tion between the Department of Justice and the Department of the Interior will likely have a favorable impact on the effectiveness of the tribal court system.

As you read, consider the following questions:

1. According to the viewpoint, what does the Tribal Law and Order Act of 2010 recognize as being directly responsible for the rise in violent crime within Indian tribes?

2. How many federally recognized tribes are there, according to the viewpoint?

3. What does the viewpoint indicate as key advantages to deputizing tribal police as federal law enforcement officers?

The Department of Justice (DOJ) has reported from the latest available data that the crime rates experienced by American Indians nationwide are two and a half times higher than those experienced by the general population in the United States. Specifically, DOJ reported that from 1992 to 2001, American Indians, nationally, experienced violent crimes at an estimated rate of 101 violent crimes per 1,000 Indians annually, which is more than twice the estimated national rate of 41 per 1,000 persons. While violent-crime rate statistics specific to Indian country are not available, the Tribal Law and Order Act of 2010 (TLOA) recognizes that Indian tribes have faced significant increases of burglary, assault, child abuse, and domestic violence as a direct result of increased methamphetamine use on Indian reservations. Further, it is estimated that 39 percent of American Indian and Alaska Native women will be subjected to domestic violence during their lifetime. Such crime levels can have a devastating effect on the quality of life for tribal communities and signal a public safety crisis in Indian country. Tribal, state, or federal governments may have jurisdiction to prosecute Indian offenders who commit crimes of a more serious nature in Indian country; however, tribal governments do not have jurisdiction to prosecute non-Indians, even if the victim is Indian. Rather, non-Indian offenders who commit crimes against Indians may be prosecuted by the federal government or, where jurisdiction has been conferred, a state government. Although TLOA acknowledges that tribal justice systems are often the most appropriate institutions for maintaining law and order in Indian country, they face challenges in effectively administering justice due to limited personnel and resources, increasing volume and complexity of criminal caseloads, and limited sentencing authority. To that end and in light of the challenges that tribes face in adjudicating crimes, tribal communities rely on the federal government to investigate and prosecute a variety of crimes in Indian country.

The Department of the Interior (DOI) and DOJ are the two primary federal agencies that provide support to federally recognized tribes to ensure safe communities in Indian country and help tribes administer justice. First, DOI, through the Bureau of Indian Affairs (BIA), provides funding to entities of the tribal justice system including tribal courts, law enforcement agencies, and detention facilities. Additionally, BIA investigates crimes that occur in Indian country, and assists tribes in their efforts to establish and maintain judicial systems, among other things. Second, within DOJ, the Federal Bureau of Investigation (FBI) conducts criminal investigations, while the U.S. Attorneys' Offices (USAO) may exercise its jurisdiction to prosecute crime in Indian country. A number of DOJ components provide grant funding, training, and technical assistance to tribes for the purpose of enhancing tribal justice systems. In 2010, DOI and DOJ announced that public safety in tribal communities is to be a priority for their respective agencies and launched a number of initiatives intended to help address tribal justice issues. Further, TLOA was signed into law on July 29, 2010, to help address the wide-ranging challenges facing tribes and improve the response to and prosecution of crime in Indian country. . . .

Criminal Justice in Indian Country

In 2004, DOJ estimated that American Indians experience rates of violent crime that are far higher than most other racial and ethnic groups in the United States. For example, DOJ estimated that across the United States, the annual average violent-crime rate among American Indians was twice as high as that of African Americans, and 2-1/2 times as high as that of whites, and 4-1/2 times as high as that of Asians. Also, domestic and sexual violence against American Indian women is among the most critical public safety challenges in Indian country, where, in some tribal communities, according to a study commissioned by DOJ, American Indian women face murder rates that are more than 10 times the national average. Oftentimes, alcohol and drug use play a significant role in violent crimes in Indian country. According to DOJ, American Indian victims reported alcohol use by 62 percent of offenders compared to 42 percent for all races.

Tribal or BIA law enforcement officers are often among the first responders to crimes on Indian reservations; however, law enforcement resources are scarce. BIA estimates that there are fewer than 3,000 tribal and BIA law enforcement officers to patrol more than 56 million acres of Indian country. According to a DOJ study, the ratio of law enforcement officers to residents in Indian country is far less than in non-tribal areas. In the study, researchers estimated that there are fewer than 2 officers per 1,000 residents in Indian country compared to a range of 3.9 to 6.6 officers per 1,000 residents in non-tribal areas such as Detroit, Michigan and Washington, D.C. The challenge of limited law enforcement resources is exacerbated by the geographic isolation or vast size of many reservations. In some instances officers may need to travel hundreds of miles to reach a crime scene. For example, the Pine

Ridge Indian Reservation in South Dakota has about 88 sworn tribal officers to serve 47,000 residents across 3,466 square miles, which equates to a ratio of 1 officer per 39 square miles of land, according to BIA.

In total there are 565 federally recognized tribes; each has unique public safety challenges based on different cultures, economic conditions, and geographic location, among other factors. These factors make it challenging to implement a uniform solution to address the public safety challenges confronting Indian country. Nonetheless, tribal justice systems are considered to be the most appropriate institutions for maintaining law and order in Indian country. Generally, tribal courts have adopted federal and state court models; however, tribal courts also strive to maintain traditional systems of adjudication such as peacemaking or sentencing circles.

Law enforcement, courts, and detention/correction programs are key components of the tribal justice system that is intended to protect tribal communities; however, each part of the system faces varied challenges in Indian country. Shortcomings and successes in one area may exacerbate problems in another area. For example, a law enforcement initiative designed to increase police presence on a reservation could result in increased arrests, thereby overwhelming a tribal court's caseload or an overcrowded detention facility. . . .

Multiple Federal Efforts Exist to Address Challenges Faced by Tribal Courts

Various federal efforts exist that could help to address some of the challenges that tribes face in effectively adjudicating crime in Indian country. For example, TLOA: (1) authorizes tribal courts to impose a term of imprisonment on certain convicted defendants in excess of 1 year; (2) authorizes and encourages USAO to appoint Special Assistant U.S. Attorneys (SAUSA), including the appointment of tribal prosecutors to assist in prosecuting federal offenses committed in Indian country; (3) requires that federal entities coordinate with appropriate tribal law enforcement and justice officials on the status of criminal investigations terminated without referral or declined prosecution; and (4) requires BOP [Federal Bureau of Prisons] to establish a pilot program to house, in federal prison, Indian offenders convicted of a violent crime in tribal court and sentenced to 2 or more years imprisonment. Additionally, to help address issues regarding judicial independence, BIA has ongoing and planned training to help increase tribes' awareness about the significance of judicial independence. Many of these initiatives directly resulted from the enactment of TLOA in July 2010; and at this time, these initiatives are in the early stages of implementation. As a result, it is too early to tell the extent to which these initiatives are helping to address the challenges that tribes face in effectively adjudicating crime in Indian country.

Various federal efforts are under way that provide additional resources to assist tribes in the investigation and prosecution of crime in Indian country including (1) additional federal prosecutors, (2) authorizing tribal courts to impose longer prison sentences on certain convicted defendants, (3) mandating changes to the program that authorizes BIA to enter into agreements to aid in law enforcement in Indian country, and (4) affording tribal prosecutors opportunities to become Special Assistant U.S. Attorneys to assist in prosecuting federal offenses committed in Indian country. First, to help address the high levels of violent crime in Indian country, in May 2010, DOJ announced the addition of 30 Assistant U.S. Attorneys (AUSA) to serve as tribal liaisons in 21 USAO district offices that contain Indian country including the four states that we visited as part of our work—Arizona, New Mexico, North Dakota, and South Dakota. According to DOJ, these additional resources will help the department work with its tribal law enforcement partners to improve public safety in Indian country. DOJ also allocated 3 additional AUSAs to help

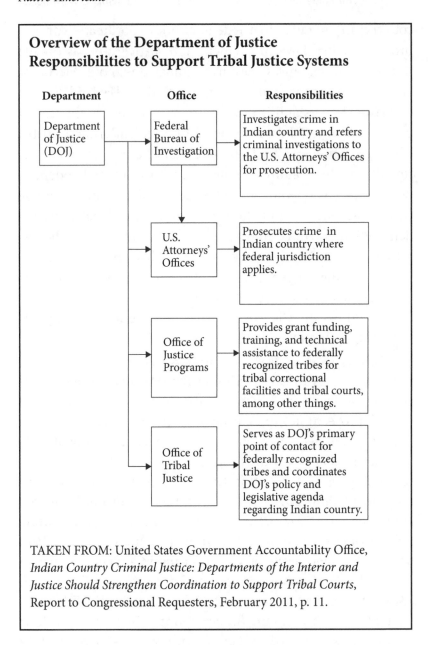

Overview of the Department of Justice Responsibilities to Support Tribal Justice Systems

Department	Office	Responsibilities
Department of Justice (DOJ)	Federal Bureau of Investigation	Investigates crime in Indian country and refers criminal investigations to the U.S. Attorneys' Offices for prosecution.
	U.S. Attorneys' Offices	Prosecutes crime in Indian country where federal jurisdiction applies.
	Office of Justice Programs	Provides grant funding, training, and technical assistance to federally recognized tribes for tribal correctional facilities and tribal courts, among other things.
	Office of Tribal Justice	Serves as DOJ's primary point of contact for federally recognized tribes and coordinates DOJ's policy and legislative agenda regarding Indian country.

TAKEN FROM: United States Government Accountability Office, *Indian Country Criminal Justice: Departments of the Interior and Justice Should Strengthen Coordination to Support Tribal Courts*, Report to Congressional Requesters, February 2011, p. 11.

support its Community Prosecution Pilot Project which it launched at two of the tribes we visited—the portion of Navajo Nation within New Mexico and the Oglala Sioux Tribe in South Dakota. Under this pilot project, the AUSAs will be assigned to work at their designated reservation on a regular basis and will work in collaboration with the tribe to develop strategies that are tailored to meet the public safety challenges facing the tribe.

Second, TLOA authorizes tribal courts to imprison convicted offenders for up to a maximum of 3 years if the defendant has been previously convicted of the same or a comparable crime in any jurisdiction (including tribal) within the United States or is being prosecuted for an offense comparable to an offense that would be punishable by more than 1 year if prosecuted in state or federal court. To impose an enhanced sentence, the defendant must be afforded the right to effective assistance of counsel and, if indigent, the assistance of a licensed attorney at the tribe's expense; a licensed judge with sufficient legal training must preside over the proceeding; prior to charging the defendant, the tribal government criminal laws and rules of evidence and criminal procedure must be made publicly available; and the tribal court must maintain a record of the criminal proceedings. Generally, tribal justice officials from 9 of the 12 tribes we visited stated that they welcome the new sentencing authority, but officials from two of the tribes noted that they would likely use the new authority on a case-by-case basis because they lacked the infrastructure to fully meet the requisite conditions. For example, the chief judge from one of the New Mexico pueblos we visited noted that rather than hiring a full-time public defender, the pueblo is considering hiring an attorney on contract to be used on a case-by-case basis when the enhanced sentencing authority may be exercised.

Enhanced Resources for Tribal Law Enforcement and Prosecutors

Third, TLOA mandates changes to the Special Law Enforcement Commission (SLEC) program which authorizes BIA to enter into agreements for the use of personnel or facilities of federal, tribal, state, or other government agencies to aid in the enforcement of federal or, with the tribe's consent, tribal law in Indian country. Specifically, within 180 days of enactment, the secretary of the interior shall develop a plan to enhance the certification and provision of special law enforcement commissions to tribal law enforcement officials, among others, that includes regional training sessions held at least biannually in Indian country to educate and certify candidates for the SLEC. The secretary of the interior, in consultation with tribes and tribal law enforcement agencies, must also develop minimum requirements to be included in SLEC agreements. Under the SLEC program, administered by the BIA, tribal police may be deputized as federal law enforcement officers, which affords them the authorities and protections available to federal law enforcement officers. According to BIA, given the potential difficulties arresting officers face in determining whether a victim or offender is an Indian or not or whether the alleged crime has occurred in Indian country (for purposes of determining jurisdiction at the time of arrest), a tribal officer deputized to enforce federal law is not charged with determining the appropriate jurisdiction for filing charges; rather this is to be determined by the prosecutor or court to which the arresting officer delivers the offender.

Lastly, among other provisions, TLOA explicitly authorizes and encourages the appointment of qualified attorneys, including tribal prosecutors, as Special Assistant U.S. Attorneys (SAUSA) to assist in the prosecution of federal offenses and administration of justice in Indian country. If appointed as a SAUSA, a tribal prosecutor may pursue in federal court an Indian country criminal matter with federal jurisdiction that, if successful, could result in the convicted defendant receiving a sentence greater than if the matter had been prosecuted in tribal court. According to the associate attorney general, many tribal prosecutors have valuable experience and expertise that DOJ can draw on to prosecute crime and enforce federal criminal law in Indian country. Further, tribal prosecutors at four of the 12 tribes we visited are in varying stages of obtaining SAUSA credentials. The chief prosecutor at a New Mexico pueblo who is in the process of obtaining a SAUSA credential cited various benefits arising from a SAUSA appointment including increased: (1) prosecution of criminal cases that involve domestic violence and child sexual abuse; (2) prosecution of misdemeanor-level offenses committed by non-Indians against Indians that occur in Indian country; (3) ability to directly present criminal investigations to the district USAO rather than solely relying on BIA criminal investigators to do so; and (4) cooperation from tribal crime victims and witnesses who may be more forthcoming with someone closely affiliated with the pueblo rather than federal investigators or prosecutors, thereby helping to facilitate a more successful investigation and prosecution of a federal crime. . . .

Strengthened Information Sharing Could Increase the Efficiency and Effectiveness of Tribal Courts

To meet their respective responsibilities to support tribal courts, BIA and DOJ provide funding, training, and technical assistance to tribal courts; however, the two agencies do not leverage each other's resources—one of the eight collaboration practices that we have identified—by sharing certain relevant information that could benefit each agency's efforts to enhance the capacity of tribal courts to effectively administer justice in Indian country. In October 2009, DOJ told the leadership of the Senate Indian Affairs Committee that it was taking action to provide better coordination with DOI to ensure that the two agencies' tribal courts initiatives are coordinated to develop and support tribal courts to help tribal courts build the capacity needed to exercise the enhanced sentencing authority proposed for tribes under TLOA. However, when we met with OJP and BIA program officials in October 2010 and

November 2010, respectively, they noted that the information sharing and coordination mechanisms that are in place to support tribal detention initiatives have not extended to tribal court initiatives. . . .

We have previously reported that collaborating agencies are most effective when they look for opportunities to leverage each other's resources, thereby obtaining benefits that may not otherwise be available if the agencies work separately. Further, *Standards for Internal Control in the Federal Government* call for agencies to enhance their effectiveness by obtaining information from external stakeholders that may have a significant impact on the agency achieving its goals. Developing mechanisms for identifying and sharing information and resources related to tribal courts could yield potential benefits in terms of leveraging efforts already under way and minimizing the potential for unnecessary duplication in federal agencies' efforts to support tribal courts. Moreover, by sharing information resources, BIA and DOJ could achieve additional benefits that result from the different levels of expertise and capacities that each agency brings. BIA and DOJ officials acknowledged that the two agencies could benefit from working together to share information and leverage resources to address the needs of tribal courts and stated that they would begin taking steps to do so.

> *"If the federal government simply abolished the [Bureau of Indian Affairs] . . . the federal government would breach one of its oldest and greatest responsibilities."*

The Bureau of Indian Affairs Serves an Important Function and Should Remain Open

Lisa Shellenberger

Lisa Shellenberger is a law clerk for the firm Smith, Shelton & Ragona, LLC, in Westminster, Colorado; a judicial fellow at the Colorado State Supreme Court; and a Juris Doctor candidate at the University of Colorado Law School. In the following viewpoint, Shellenberger maintains that the Bureau of Indian Affairs (BIA) is a vitally important agency that not only provides much-needed assistance and services to Native Americans but also represents a promise made by the federal government two centuries ago granting sovereignty and guardianship to all tribal nations. Shellenberger takes issue with commentator John Stossel's calls to abolish the BIA, arguing that to do so would break the government's promise and condemn struggling tribes to abject

Lisa Shellenberger, "The Reasoning for and Purpose of the Bureau of Indian Affairs—Enlightening Journalist John Stossel," Smith, Shelton & Ragona, LLC, April 2011. Reproduced by permission of the author.

poverty and death. The author explains the history behind the BIA and the dire consequences that occurred in the past when the government failed in its support of many tribes. Furthermore, Shellenberger asserts, even if some tribes are financially equipped to fund their own services, those tribes are still as legally entitled to federal funding as tribes that are impoverished.

As you read, consider the following questions:

1. What phrase did the Supreme Court use to describe the sovereignty of tribal governments, according to Shellenberger?

2. In which government department is the Bureau of Indian Affairs located, according to the viewpoint?

3. What answer does Shellenberger offer to the question of why the Bureau of Indian Affairs still exists?

Congress, American presidents, the United States Supreme Court, and the States have all, in many varied ways, given recognition to Native American tribes as sovereign entities. Sovereign tribal authority is inherent to Indian tribes and predates any other form of law in this country. It is recognized in enduring constitutional principles, and the Supreme Court has explicitly confirmed that the United States Constitution acknowledges the status of tribes as nations. Due to their sovereign, national status, tribes are political entities; they are not racial groups. Therefore, the federal and state governments must deal with tribes differently. The key principle here is that tribes' political status is the fundamental difference between Indian Nations and other groups of people within the United States, such as African Americans, as [journalist] John Stossel suggested. This critical and unique distinction between tribes and other groups of people is a crucial factor that Mr. Stossel, and unfortunately most Americans, is missing.

Stossel's commentary questioning the purpose of the Bureau of Indian Affairs ("BIA") is ignorant of an important principle grounded in centuries of American history, custom, and law: Indian tribes have a historic and special relationship with the federal government. At its broadest, the special relationship between the tribes and the federal government includes the mixture of legal duties, moral obligations, understandings and expectancies that have arisen over the course of over 235 years of dealings between the federal government and tribes. In its narrowest sense, the relationship approximates that of trustee and beneficiary, with the trustee (the United States) subject to a degree of legally enforceable responsibilities.

Tribal Sovereignty and Federal Trust Responsibility

This special relationship exists due to the nature of the two assemblies being separate sovereigns, but with tribal sovereignty existing under the umbrella of federal sovereignty. This apparent hierarchy exists because the Supreme Court declared Indian Nations to be "domestic dependent nations," with a relationship to the United States like that of a ward to a guardian. Due to their nation status, the federal government and the states have been entering into legally enforceable contracts with tribes for centuries. These agreements have been and are still made with the understanding that tribes are separate political bodies. The American government has never acknowledged any other groups' political power, sovereignty, or national presence within the United States.

While illustrative of tribal sovereignty and the trust relationship owed by the federal government, treaties have not always been positive agreements for American Indians. For the layman, treaties are much like contracts. Tribes put up substantial considerations for the services they are receiving now from the federal government. The loss of countless Indian lives, the unilateral taking of millions of acres of land, the willful degradation and attempted eradication of Indian cultures, and the stripping and taking of tribal natural resources and food were all actions taken by the U.S government to satisfy its greed and an equally greedy and fearful American populace. Nonetheless, these sacrifices were made in exchange for "considerations" that the tribes were to receive from the federal government, including federal oversight, assistance, and protection. While many of the treaties were drafted over two hundred years ago, the United States is still bound by its word, and as a result—much like a contract for services—the enforceability of treaties remains sound.

The BIA's Role and Purpose

The primary instrument for carrying out the federal trust responsibility has been the Bureau of Indian Affairs, located for the past one hundred fifty years within the Department of the Interior. The bureau has evolved into a complex bureaucracy of many thousands of employees, which includes twelve area offices and eighty-odd agencies located on reservation lands. The most substantial activities of the bureau today are education and the management of tribal resources, particularly lands. Examples of other activities are the administration of bureau housing programs, building and maintenance of roads, licensing of Indian traders, provision of emergency relief, and the administration of various grant programs. The BIA's initial paternalistic role is fading, and today the emphasis of federal policy is upon encouraging tribal self-determination, and the bureau has certainly receded from monolithic control of tribal affairs. Additionally, many of the bureau's management functions have been contracted to the tribes under the Indian Self-Determination and Education Assistance Act of 1975.

Stossel boldly, yet with tragic ignorance, argues for the bureau's abolition without any regard for the consequences. Many, like Stossel, may contemplate why the Bureau of Indian Affairs still exists if tribal self-determination is the goal. The answer is that the Bureau of Indian Affairs still exists because

The Important Functions of the Bureau of Indian Affairs

[The Bureau of] Indian Affairs offers an extensive scope of programs that covers the entire range of federal, state and local government services. Programs administered ... through the Bureau of Indian Education (BIE) include an education system consisting of 183 schools and dormitories educating approximately 42,000 elementary and secondary students and 28 tribal colleges, universities, and postsecondary schools. Programs administered through the Bureau of Indian Affairs (BIA) include social services, natural resources management on trust lands representing 55 million surface acres and 57 million acres of subsurface minerals estates, economic development programs in some of the most isolated and economically depressed areas of the United States, law enforcement and detention services, administration of tribal courts, implementation of land and water claim settlements, housing improvement, disaster relief, replacement and repair of schools, repair and maintenance of roads and bridges, and the repair of structural deficiencies on high-hazard dams. The BIA operates a series of irrigation systems and provides electricity to rural parts of Arizona.

Through Indian Affairs programs, tribes improve their tribal government infrastructure, community infrastructure, education, job training, and employment opportunities along with other components of long-term sustainable development that work to improve the quality of life for their members.

"What We Do,"
US Department of the Interior: Indian Affairs, 2011.
www.bia.gov.

it was bargained for by the tribes. Countless treaties, executive orders, and agreements between tribes and the United States provided that the federal government would indefinitely be bound to a federal trust responsibility, which includes the administration of a number of programs for tribes. The BIA is seen as the embodiment of the federal trust responsibility. And while tribes may face difficulties with tribal autonomy and self-determination due to the existence of the bureau, the suggestion of abolition inevitably encounters opposition from the tribes.

Tribes have structured their reservations, laws, and governments to account for the federal government oversight to which they acquiesced and the assistance for which they bargained. If the federal government simply abolished the BIA, as Stossel advocates, the federal government would breach one of its oldest and greatest responsibilities. An attempt to end the BIA is perceived as an attempt to do away with the trust relationship itself—in other words, to "terminate." Termination is akin to genocide [deliberate murder of an ethnic, racial, political, cultural, or national group]. Of course, this has already been tried in the history of federal-tribal relations. The experience of the tribes whose relationship with the federal government was terminated in the 1950s was sufficiently dismal that any hint of the policy's revival triggers instant opposition. Tribes would once again suffer greatly, and not because they are unable to survive without federal government assistance, but because they have rightfully relied on a partnership with the federal government for many years. With this partnership, tribes have chartered countless successful businesses, creating whole Indian economies, some of which have expanded into international markets. So while some tribes still need federal assistance and some do not, all are legally entitled to it.

Before John Stossel makes another bold statement regarding what he thinks about the BIA, he may want to first reference and understand centuries of American Indian history and law.

> "As long as there exists a Bureau of Indian Affairs, American Indians will remain poor, broken and without freedom."

The Bureau of Indian Affairs Is Corrupt and Dysfunctional and Should Be Eliminated

Zach Einterz

Zach Einterz has contributed several articles to University Wire. *In the following viewpoint, Einterz advocates abolishing the Bureau of Indian Affairs (BIA), citing a history of policies that serve government and corporate interests at the expense of Native Americans' rights and general welfare. He argues that many of the BIA's activities are illegal because they violate tribal sovereignty, such as when the federal government grants mineral rights to corporations rather than to Native American landowners. The BIA has been so grossly mismanaged and corrupted, Einterz insists, that it has condemned Native Americans to a life of disenfranchisement and poverty. The only means of freeing Native Americans to improve their situation, according to Einterz, is to disband the BIA and give tribes full authority and power to govern themselves.*

Zach Einterz, "Abolish the Bureau of Indian Affairs," *The Observer* (Notre Dame), February 20, 2007. Reproduced by permission.

As you read, consider the following questions:

1. According to the viewpoint, under which government department was the Bureau of Indian Affairs originally organized?

2. What amount of money does the Bureau of Indian Affairs owe to Indian trust funds, according to the lawsuit known as *Cobell vs. Kempthorne*, as cited in the viewpoint?

3. How much higher than the national average are suicide rates among Native Americans, according to the author?

"Let me be a free man,
free to travel, free to stop,
free to work, free to trade where I
choose,
free to choose my own teachers,
free to follow the religion of my
fathers,
free to talk, think and act for my-
self
—and I will obey every law or submit to the penalty."

—*Chief Joseph of the Nez Perce*

Thanksgiving is not unique to America. Traditional celebrations of the autumnal harvest are celebrated in many cultures and countries. However, in America, Thanksgiving takes on a special meaning as we remember some of the first celebrants of Thanksgiving in the New World, the Pilgrims. Facing religious persecution in their homeland, the Pilgrims fled England and a tyrannical King James for the promise of the New World. Thus, Thanksgiving is not just a celebration of the year's harvest, but also a reminder of the promise of freedom in America.

At the same time that most Americans will be celebrating Thanksgiving, there will be a small group of citizens protesting at Plymouth Rock. Every year since 1970, American Indians and their supporters have been gathering at Plymouth Rock to observe their "National Day of Mourning." These Indians are the other half of the Thanksgiving story. While the European colonizers prospered freely and built our great country, the Indians suffered and died, often at the hands of our own government. I should not need to give a detailed history of American Indian abuses perpetuated by the United States people and its government. We all know the story. However, as if past atrocities were not enough, the federal government continues today to persecute Native Americans under the Bureau of Indian Affairs.

A History of Patronizing Policies, Abuse and Neglect

The bureau was created (indeed, all existing government bureaucracies were created) because politicians in Washington believed that they knew what was best for a group of individuals. Originally organized under the War Department, the bureau was responsible for removing Indians from their homelands and placing them on unproductive reservations. Then the bureau created government schools where they sent Indian children to be "civilized." Civilized in this case means they were abused, forbidden to speak their native tongue, separated from family and purged of any native cultural education. Then the bureau overlooked traditional Indian views of communal property and divided reservation lands into individual plots. This was all purported to be in the Indians' best interest because it would allow them to assimilate faster into the European way of life.

The bureau continues to this day to unlawfully meddle in the affairs of American Indians. It gives federal recognition and gaming rights to some tribes while spurning others. It in-

The Bureau of Indian Affairs Is a Criminal Enterprise

There are no "Indian" casinos. There are no "Indian" reservations. The Indian tribes are our pupils and our wards by order of the United States Supreme Court. The American Indian tribes do not hold title to their lands. The taxpayers have held their title in abeyance since the Bureau of Indian Affairs was empowered unlawfully by Congress and the executive branch in 1831. There insurrection over the majority opinion of the Supreme Court gave birth to an ethnic cleansing program that is still operating today as a shameless criminal empire; the BIA reservation system. . . .

Therefore, there are only "BIA" syndicate owned casinos, and they are all located within "BIA" syndicate reservations; both are under the absolute control of the government. To imply that anything within the BIA's crime sanctuaries is owned or controlled by the "Indians" is merely furthering the fraud and subterfuge that is the Indian Affairs bureaucracy.

Harold Lee,
"The Bureau of Indian Affairs (America's True Evil Empire),"
International Card and Game Players Association (ICGPA),
April 18, 2011. www.icgpa.org.

tervenes in the affairs of tribal governance and dictates tribal policies. It administers health and education programs that are woefully inadequate. As with any government agency, the bureau is prone to corruption and mismanagement.

After the allotment of reservation lands to individual Indians, many Indians placed their lands in a trust. The bureau was in charge of managing this land trust, contracting out mineral and resource rights to private companies. Many of these contracts heavily favored the corporations at the expense of the American Indian landowners.

Furthermore, the funds from the sale of these rights have been incredibly mismanaged. In 1996, American Indian rights groups sued the Department of the Interior and the bureau. The case, *Cobell v. Kempthorne* [also known as *Cobell v. Salazar*], claims that the bureau owes more than $13 billion to the Indian trusts funds. According to Judge Royce Lamberth, "The actions of Interior and Secretary [Gale Ann] Norton in this instance again demonstrate why the court continues to believe that Interior sets the gold standard for mismanagement of a government agency."

Rampant Corruption

The bureau is also a breeding ground for corruption. It was the competition for lucrative Indian gaming contracts that started Jack Abramoff on his road to infamy.

So what has the American Indian gained from the corruption, mismanagement and "in-your-best-interest" government programs? American Indian suicide rates are 1.5 times the national average. Rates of poverty and unemployment are more than twice the national average. Is it just a coincidence that the poorest people in our nation are also subjected to the most government oversight? Certainly not. Freedom breeds prosperity. Rather than lifting American Indians out of poverty, the bureau has fostered it through years of corruption, mismanagement and patronization.

As we commemorate Native American History Month next November, let us remember that the struggle for American Indian sovereignty is not over. Critics of the bureau are not few and far between, and many American Indians have called for the abolishment of the bureau. As long as there exists a Bureau of Indian Affairs, American Indians will remain poor, broken and without freedom. It is time to let American Indians rule themselves. Restore their property, their rights, and their sovereignty. Let them decide for themselves what is best for their people, their culture and their prosperity.

| "Abolish the Bureau of Indian Affairs, the Indian Health Service, and all other federal agencies that serve Native American interests. These agencies have outlived whatever usefulness they had."

The Bureau of Indian Affairs Should Be Closed to Save Taxpayer Money

Carl Horowitz

Carl Horowitz is a conservative political commentator and columnist, as well as the director of the Organized Labor Accountability Project of the National Legal and Policy Center. In the following viewpoint, Horowitz calls for dismantling the Bureau of Indian Affairs (BIA), as well as all other federal agencies devoted to the concerns of Native Americans, and begin moving toward assimilating Native Americans into mainstream American society. He maintains that the sovereign status afforded to tribal governments encourages corruption and criminal activity, both of which he declares are rampant within tribal leadership. Horowitz also decries what he characterizes as class-action lawsuits based on shaky premises that are designed to squeeze taxpayer money out of various government agencies. Unethical and

Carl Horowitz, "No Reservations: The Case for Dismantling the Indian Bureaucracy," Townhall.com, February 4, 2011. Reproduced by permission of the author.

criminal lobbying activity, Horowitz asserts, combined with what he describes as "Indian identity politics" and a separatist mind-set, exacerbate and capitalize on an already dysfunctional system that erodes America's national identity.

As you read, consider the following questions:

1. What year was the Bureau of Indian Affairs established and by whom, according to Horowitz?

2. What right was granted to Indian tribes under the Indian Gaming Regulatory Act, according to the viewpoint?

3. A period of "Indian identity politics" culminated in Congress passing which two laws in the 1970s, according to Horowitz?

If ever a federal agency were a candidate for termination, the Bureau of Indian Affairs (BIA) would make for a good choice. The BIA combines patronage and ethnic separatism into a single package, wasting sizable tax dollars in the process. Yet few in Congress have the stomach for a fight with supporters of the bureau, now with a roughly $2.7 billion annual budget. That's not the only Indian agency in need of serious downsizing.

A Flawed System

The Bureau of Indian Affairs actually goes back nearly two centuries. Secretary of War John Calhoun virtually single-handedly created the BIA in 1824 to oversee treaty negotiations, conduct trade, establish budgets, and operate schools. In 1849, Congress moved the bureau from the War Department to the new Interior Department, where it since has been housed. In recent decades, the agency has become a conduit through which tribal leaders and their allies can accrue money and influence. It's a variation on what public choice economists call "regulatory capture," in which firms—especially large ones—effectively dictate policies and practices to the regulator, so as to maximize competitive advantage.

The current system is a by-product of periodic warfare beginning in the early 17th century and lasting through most of the 19th century. There are now 565 federally recognized Indian (including Alaskan) tribes in this land of ours, representing nearly two million persons. Indian territories comprise some 55 million surface acres. Crucially, a tribe operates under a federal grant of sovereign status. Taken as a whole, Indian tribes are a loose confederacy of mini-nations, each with its own elected tribal government overseeing courts, schools, job training, health care, infrastructure development, and on due occasion, casinos.

Widespread Corruption and Theft

Within their respective reservations, tribal leaders enjoy enormous power. Too often, they and employees use this power as a cover for corruption. Recent cases abound. At the Fort Peck Indian Reservation in northeastern Montana, for example, six office employees—two federal and four tribal—pleaded guilty last year [2010] to embezzling roughly $400,000 from a tribal credit program. In Oklahoma, Dawena Pappan, former secretary-treasurer for the Tonkawa tribe, pleaded guilty in federal court that year to stealing hundreds of thousands of dollars in casino proceeds with help from other Tonkawa officers.

Want more? Emily Anne Saupitty, secretary-treasurer of the Apache of Oklahoma, was found guilty by a federal jury of embezzling $46,068 in oil and gas royalty taxes, though her actual thefts amounted to nearly $108,000. Evelyn James, former president of the San Juan Southern Paiute tribe in Arizona, pleaded guilty to theft and money laundering of nearly $300,000 in Justice Department community policing funds. And about a dozen persons, including two former tribal officials, pleaded guilty or were found guilty in Oklahoma City federal court to embezzling about $750,000 from the Lucky Star Casinos, operated by the Cheyenne and Arapaho of Oklahoma.

It isn't just Bureau of Indian Affairs funds that have made their way into the pockets of crooks. In mid-2008, for example, the Government Accountability Office (GAO) issued a report revealing that the Indian Health Service (IHS), part of the Department of Health and Human Services, during fiscal years 2004–07 "lost" about 5,000 pieces of medical equipment with an acquisition value of $15.8 million. In a follow-up evaluation audit released in June 2009, the GAO noted: "IHS continues to lose property at an alarming rate, reporting lost or stolen property with an acquisition value of about $3.5 million in a little over a year. . . ." Missing items included a $170,000 ultrasound unit, a $100,795 mammography X-ray machine, and various dental chairs and diagnostic monitors.

Lawsuits and Gaming Generate Major Revenue

Far bigger piles of loot, however, can be made legally. Class action lawsuits are one route. Over the past few months, Indian plaintiffs and their attorneys managed to coax massive settlements from the federal government in two long-standing unrelated civil suits. Last October, lawyers for tens of thousands of Indians corralled a $760 million agreement from the U.S. Department of Agriculture as compensation for credit discrimination against Native American farmers and ranchers. Known as *Keepseagle v. Vilsack* and originally filed by a Sioux couple in North Dakota in 1999 as a copycat of the *Pigford* [referring to *Pigford v. Glickman*] (i.e., "black farmer") lawsuit, the case did not uncover any specific acts of willful discrimination. In the other lawsuit, Congress in November created a $3.4 billion trust fund to be shared by an estimated 300,000 to 500,000 Indians, pursuant to the settlement in *Cobell v. Salazar* [also known as *Cobell v. Kempthorne*], in which the plaintiffs had alleged that the Interior Department for decades had squandered royalties due individual Indians for extracted oil, gas, timber and other natural resources from tribal lands. The details of the case suggest a well-planned and -executed plaintiff shakedown.

An even bigger street-legal money maker is casino gambling. In 1988, Congress enacted and President [Ronald] Reagan signed the Indian Gaming Regulatory Act (IGRA), which recognized "the right of Indian tribes in the United States to establish gambling and gaming facilities on their reservations as long as the states in which they are located have some form of legalized gambling." This legislation effectively conferred monopoly rights upon a tribe to operate a casino on its property, subject to regulation by the National Indian Gaming Commission. These enterprises are immune from state regulation. Moreover, they are exempt from federal income taxation, though state governments may tax a portion of slot machine revenues.

Currently, some 220 recognized Native American tribes operate a combined roughly 400 Class I, II and III (casinos fit under the latter category) gaming facilities. Given the seemingly limitless capacity of Americans to place wagers, this has meant big bucks. The Foxwoods Resort Casino in southeastern Connecticut, owned by the Mashantucket Western Pequot Tribal Nation, thanks to several expansions, has become the largest hotel-casino complex in the U.S. Featuring 7,200 slot machines and 380 table games, the luxury facility takes in roughly $1.5 billion annually from combined gaming and non-gaming sources. Right down the road is the nation's second-largest casino venue, the Mohegan Sun Resort & Casino. Owned by the Mohegan tribe, this high-end getaway destination features 300,000 square feet of gaming space within three casinos. The Pechanga Resort and Casino in Temecula, California, isn't exactly small time either, containing 200,000 square feet of gaming space and 3,400 slot machines.

All told, Indian gaming in 2009 took in $26.5 billion in revenues. This represents an explosive increase from $100 million in 1988, the year of IGRA passage.

Unscrupulous Lobbying and Identity Politics

Someone out there is getting rich. And it isn't just tribal leaders and outside investors. Tribes operate with a grant of monopoly privilege. Remaining shielded from competition requires gaining access to federal and state legislators to vote the right way. That's where lobbyists come in. The 2006 final report of the Senate Indian Affairs Committee, chaired by John McCain, R-Ariz., revealed that Jack Abramoff, though an extreme example (hence, the superficially satisfying cliché, "disgraced lobbyist Jack Abramoff"), was part of a larger "come and get it" political culture. A former BIA official, Wayne Smith, grandson of a Sioux chief, explained to CBS News at the time: "I had lobbyists . . . tell me that 'It was our time, this is our time to make some money in the Indian game arena. We worked hard to get this president elected, and we expect to be rewarded for it.'" What matters here is that influence-buying is a product of tribal sovereignty and monopoly privilege. "Lobbyists"—love them or hate them—will always be around to service an Indian client's political needs under this scenario.

If all this theft and influence-peddling amounted to nothing more than a few anecdotes, it would be easy to minimize their importance. Such behavior can be found in any type of organization, whether government agencies, corporations, unions, philanthropies or churches. Yet these cases, in fact, represent a fraction of widespread criminal and otherwise ethically challenged activity. It is hard to avoid the conclusion that the system of tribal governance, with an able assist from Washington, is dysfunctional.

Bureaucratic client capture offers a partial explanation for this state of affairs. The ultimate problem is the setting aside of territory and public funds to accommodate Indian "nations." Indian identity politics, at bottom, is about irredentism—the condition of two or more ethnic, linguistic or religious groups claiming sovereignty over the same territory. Many Indians have a deep attachment to ancient lands they believe were stolen by the white man. The federal government can't bottle up their sense of moral entitlement. But it doesn't have to subsidize it either.

Despite our best efforts, separatism and corruption appear to have become more pronounced over the past few decades. The late Sixties and early Seventies witnessed the aggressive rise of Indian identity politics, culminating in passage by Congress of the Indian Self-Determination and Educational Assistance Act (1975) and the Indian Child Welfare Act (1978). Lawmakers further encouraged decentralization of authority in 1991 with the Tribal Self-Governance Demonstration Project Act. With larger budgets and fewer strings attached, opportunities for corruption have increased, especially as the BIA itself has come to be heavily staffed by Indian activists.

Ending the network of incestuous relationships and accompanying corruption requires that Congress do the unthinkable: Abolish the Bureau of Indian Affairs, the Indian Health Service and all other federal agencies that serve Native American interests. These agencies have outlived whatever usefulness they had. Lawmakers also ought to end the practice of formal tribal recognition. Why should Cheyenne, Choctaw, Mohawk or Sioux sovereign "nations" exist within our borders, any more than Dutch, Irish, Italian or Polish ethnic ones? It is one thing for members of a particular tribe to live in close proximity, preferring their own company. It is entirely another for Americans as a whole to be coerced into subsidizing this tribal confederacy, an arrangement that is not only costly, but also corrosive of national identity.

Back in the late 1940s, Congress set up a commission on executive branch reorganization, chaired by former president Herbert Hoover. Among its hundreds of recommendations, the Hoover Commission concluded that assimilation of Indians into the mainstream of American society must be a top priority. More than six decades later, our nation remains a long way from realizing that goal. Dismantling the Indian bureaucracy would be a major step in that direction.

> "[The National Congress of American Indians] supports swift passage of the Tribal Law and Order Act . . . to address the critical shortcomings in federal support for tribal criminal justice."

The Tribal Law and Order Act Closes a Substantial Legal Loophole

Marcus Levings

Marcus Levings served as the chairman of the Mandan, Hidatsa and Arikara Nation from 2006 to 2010, and was the 2010 Great Plains regional vice president for the National Congress of American Indians (NCAI). In the following viewpoint, Levings describes what he and the NCAI view as the tremendous potential offered by the Tribal Law and Order Act to ensure that tribal governments have crucial federal resources and authorities at their disposal to combat and prosecute crimes committed in Indian territory. Levings chronicles the grim crime statistics that plague Native American communities and notes that because of failed federal law enforcement response, crime rates have doubled

Marcus Levings, "Testimony of Marcus Levings, Great Plains Regional Vice President, National Congress of American Indians and Chairman, Mandan, Arikara and Hidatsa Nation," House of Representatives Committee on the Judiciary Oversight Hearing on H.R. 1924, The Tribal Law & Order Act of 2009, December 10, 2009, pp. 1–7.

and tripled in these communities while rates for the same crimes have fallen in other, non–Native American low-income areas. Levings details a history of the federal government ignoring Native American public safety and wellness needs and uses the falling numbers of federally prosecuted crimes in Indian country to support this contention. The Tribal Law and Order Act, Levings declares, is a crucial, urgently needed, and long-overdue step toward ensuring that tribal public safety efforts are properly supported with federal resources.

As you read, consider the following questions:

1. What did former US attorney Margaret Chiara say was the attitude of other Justice Department employees toward her interest in Native American communities' public safety concerns, according to the viewpoint?

2. Federal prosecutors declined to prosecute what portion of felony cases in Indian country over a ten-year period, according to a *Denver Post* article quoted in the viewpoint?

3. What does the viewpoint state is the percentage of crimes committed on reservations that are drug or alcohol related?

Native Americans are victims of violent crime at rates more than double those of any other demographic in the United States. One-third of our women will be raped in their lifetimes. Crime rates have been increasing in Indian country while they have been falling in similarly low-income communities throughout the United States. Nearly 10 years ago, in October 1997, the Executive Committee for Indian Country Law Enforcement Improvements issued its final report to the attorney general and the secretary of the interior. The report concluded that "there is a public safety crisis in Indian Country."

These public safety problems have existed for many decades, continue today and are the result of decades of gross under-funding for tribal criminal justice systems, a painfully complex jurisdictional scheme, and a centuries-old failure by the federal government to fulfill its public safety obligations on Indian lands. Although there have been many federal reports and studies of these problems, Congress has rarely been able to address them. Too often, the policy community has taken an ideological approach to the federal criminal laws affecting Indian people and has been unable to find common ground.

With this legislation [Tribal Law and Order Act, also known as H.R. 1924, signed into law July 29, 2010], Indian tribes and the legislative sponsors have taken a different approach. All agree that the crime statistics from Indian communities are shocking and unacceptable. Lives are at stake, and we have a duty to find solutions and move swiftly to implement those solutions. For two and a half years, NCAI [National Congress of American Indians] has worked in a bipartisan fashion with the Senate Committee on Indian Affairs and the Senate Judiciary Committee. This legislation has been well vetted and we have achieved a remarkable degree of consensus on solutions that will go a long way toward addressing these problems. Congress has a unique opportunity to reverse the regrettable public safety trends that have existed on Indian lands for far too long. . . .

A Lack of Federal Accountability

Under the Major Crimes Act and other federal laws, the federal government has the sole authority for investigation and prosecution of violent crimes and other felonies committed on Indian reservations. Despite these laws and the federal trust obligation to protect Indian communities, the violent crime rate on Indian reservations is two and a half times the national average, Indian women are victims of rape and sexual assault at three times the national average, and tribal lands are increasingly the target of drug trafficking and gang-related activity. These crime rates have been doubling and tripling in Indian country while crime rates have been falling in similarly low-income communities throughout the United States. Something is seriously wrong with the federal law enforcement response.

In the past, there has been a serious concern that the Department of Justice places no priority on addressing crime in tribal communities, and is subject to no oversight or accountability on its performance in this area. Those concerns are not unfounded. In December of 2006, the [President George W.] Bush administration fired seven U.S. attorneys, five of whom served on the attorney general's Native American Issues Subcommittee and were viewed favorably by the tribes and their respective jurisdictions. One of those individuals, former U.S. Attorney for the Western District of Michigan Margaret Chiara, openly admitted that employees within the Justice Department frowned upon her attentiveness to Indian country crime. She recounted that "[p]eople thought it was too much of my time and that it was too small of a population."

In addition, what little hard data is available supports the theory that crime on Indian lands has not been a priority for the Department of Justice. Funding for U.S. attorneys' offices has nearly doubled since 1998, yet the number of federal prosecutions of Indian country crimes has actually fallen 26 percent since 2003. These are not partisan concerns and are not confined to any one administration. In November, 2007, the *Denver Post* reported that "over the past 10 years, U.S. attorneys have declined to prosecute nearly two-thirds of felony Indian Country cases nationally."

This lack of accountability would not present a problem if tribes had some other form of recourse. However, when it comes to non-Indian offenders, tribal governments have no authority to prosecute, and they have only limited misdemeanor penal authority over Indians. In short, Indian tribes do not wish to "federalize" more crimes and put more Indians in federal prison. However, dangerous criminals that commit felonies on Indian lands—whether Indian or non-Indian—are under the sole jurisdiction of the Department of Justice and the department must not ignore its responsibility to bring them to justice. The proposed reforms in H.R. 1924 would help ensure that Indian country crime is subject to consistent and focused attention. . . .

Empowerment of Tribal Law Enforcement

Criminal jurisdiction in Indian country is divided among federal, tribal, and state governments, depending on the location of the crime, the type of crime, the race of the perpetrator, and the race of the victim. This "jurisdictional maze" is the result of over 200 years of federal legislation and Supreme Court precedent, and it creates significant impediments to law enforcement in Indian country. Each criminal investigation involves a cumbersome procedure to establish who has jurisdiction over the case based on: the nature of the offense committed, the identity of the offender, the identity of the victim, and the legal status of the land where the crime took place—none of which are consistently easy to determine.

Tribal law enforcement officers are usually the first responders to crime scenes on Indian lands, but their limited jurisdictional authority often prevents them from arresting the alleged perpetrators. Instead, their only option is to hold individuals until local, state, or federal law enforcement officers arrive, which is a difficult task—and not always successful—given the remoteness of Indian reservations and the poor coordination between government bodies.

> Section 301 [of the Tribal Law and Order Act] would go a long way toward eliminating barriers to law enforcement in Indian country. Special law enforcement commissions have long been available to tribal police, but the BIA [Bureau of

Indian Affairs] has withheld the training and granting of commissions for bureaucratic reasons. This section expands the special law enforcement commissions program, clarifies the standards required of tribal officers, and permits flexibility in reaching MOUs [memorandum of understanding] between the BIA and tribal governments that seek special commissions. Section 301 also addresses a severe problem that tribes face in recruiting and training police officers. Instead of insisting all BIA police officers receive training from the lone Indian Police Academy in Artesia, New Mexico, it allows tribal law enforcement personnel to obtain training at various state or local facilities, so long as the selected facility meets the appropriate peace officer standards of training.

Another significant concern for tribal governments is their inability to impose sentences proportionate to the crimes committed. When U.S. attorneys . . . decline to prosecute felonies in Indian country, that responsibility falls to the tribes, despite their limited sentencing power. In an oversight hearing on tribal courts and the administration of justice in Indian country held by the Senate Committee on Indian Affairs on July 24, 2008, the Honorable Theresa Pouley, Tulalip Tribal Court judge and president of the Northwest Tribal Court Judges Association, testified that, "The reality on the ground is that tribal courts are often responsible for prosecuting felony crimes." She is a prime example—during her tenure as a tribal judge, she has presided over "cases involving charges of rape, child sexual assault, drug trafficking, aggravated assault and serious domestic violence." Judge Pouley went on to express her concern that tribal courts' lack of sentencing authority was placing the tribal community at risk. Those views are echoed by tribal leaders across the United States.

Section 304 would extend tribal sentencing limitations under the Indian Civil Rights Act to provide for appropriate sentences for more serious offenders. Current law restricts tribal sentencing authority to 1 year imprisonment, a $5000 fine, or both. Yet, a 2003 report of the Native American Advisory Group to the U.S. Sentencing Guidelines Commission points out the disparity between tribal sentencing authority and the sentences that are imposed by the federal government for crimes committed under the Major Crimes Act. Assaults comprise the greatest percentage of crimes prosecuted under the Major Crimes Act, and the average federal sentence for Indians prosecuted for assault is 3.3 years. As such, there is a large gap between the maximum sentencing authority of tribes and the average sentence for the least serious crime that is prosecuted by the federal government. Section 304 would help remedy this problem by increasing tribal sentencing authority to a term of 3 years in prison, a fine of $15,000, or both. Note, however, that if a tribe subjects a defendant to a crime that is punishable by more than one year in prison, H.R. 1924 ensures protection of defendants' civil rights by requiring the tribe to provide licensed defense counsel.

The effectiveness of tribal law enforcement is further hindered by tribes' lack of access to criminal history information, including national databases such as the National Crime Information Center (NCIC), which provides criminal history data that is critical to effective law enforcement in tribal communities. NCIC is a centralized database of criminal information that interfaces with various local, state, tribal, federal, and international criminal justice systems, and has been labeled by Congress as "the single most important avenue of cooperation among law enforcement agencies."

But the problem doesn't stop there: Most tribal law enforcement authorities lack access to the entire array of criminal justice data systems that are necessary to accomplish traditional policing activities. For example, access to the NCIC requires access to the National Law Enforcement Telecommunications System (NLETS), which is the platform by which all criminal justice data files are entered, transmitted, and accessed. NLETS not only facilitates access to NCIC, but to other criminal databases that are, likewise, critical to effective law enforcement, including the Integrated Automated Fingerprint Identification System (IAFIS) and the National Instant Criminal Background Check System (NICS). Denial of full access to these basic information-sharing networks prevents tribal officers from fulfilling the most routine duties, like accessing stolen property information or running fingerprint scans, placing them and the communities they serve in grave danger.

> For the above reasons, section 303 of H.R. 1924 is critically important. This section grants tribes direct access to federal criminal information databases. It allows tribal authorities to obtain data from, as well as enter data into, these information systems, so long as they meet the applicable federal or state requirements.

NCAI strongly supports these proposals that will help empower tribal law enforcement officers.

Reauthorization of Critical Tribal Justice Programs

In theory, the federal policy of tribal self-determination has made it legally possible for tribes to carry out their inherent rights as sovereign nations to develop and manage their own comprehensive justice systems for themselves. But in practice, the federal government has repeatedly failed to provide tribes the resources necessary to create a strong law enforcement infrastructure in tribal communities. Increasing law enforcement funding is a top priority. As such, NCAI supports the efforts of H.R. 1924 to reauthorize important tribal justice programs. Title IV of the bill is central to this effort.

- Section 401 reauthorizes the Indian Alcohol and Substance Abuse Prevention and Treatment Act of 1986, taking heed of the fact that more than 80% of reservation crime is drug or alcohol related. This act provides treatment for juveniles and adults alike but emphasizes the importance of juvenile programs through the cre-

The Tribal Law and Order Act Provides Vital Protections and Services

While there will be no simple or quick fix, this comprehensive legislation [Tribal Law and Order Act, H.R. 1924] is a step in the right direction. Native American families, like all families, deserve to live in safe communities with the critical law enforcement protection and services that are standard in nearly every town and city across the country. By passing this legislation, we'll make important strides in improving law enforcement in Indian Country.

Representative Stephanie Herseth Sandlin,
Written Testimony, H.R. 1924,
Tribal Law and Order Act of 2009, House Judiciary
Subcommittee on Crime, Terrorism, and Homeland Security,
December 10, 2009.

ation of summer programs for tribal youth and the funding of emergency shelters, halfway homes, and juvenile detention centers.

- Section 403 reauthorizes and amends the tribal Community Oriented Policing (COPS) program to provide a long-term, flexible grant program for tribal governments.

- Section 404 reauthorizes the Tribal Jails program and provides for use of funds to construct tribal justice centers, including tribal jails and court buildings. It also permits funds to be used for proposed alternatives to incarceration, which is crucial, especially for those tribal justice systems whose sentencing and rehabilitation methods may not align with traditional notions of American justice.

- Section 406 is particularly important to support the development of the juvenile justice programs in Indian country. It reauthorizes and strengthens the DOJ's Tribal Youth Program and moves it to Title V of the Juvenile Justice and Delinquency Prevention Act.

In order to address the profound public safety needs in tribal communities, the additional law enforcement and criminal justice resources provided for by these provisions are badly needed.

Urgent Passage of the Tribal Law and Order Act Is Needed

NCAI supports swift passage of the Tribal Law and Order Act in the 111th Congress to address the critical shortcomings in federal support for tribal criminal justice. This is not some ill-conceived bill, thrown together at the last second to address the law enforcement needs of tribal communities. Rather, it is the product of more than two years of background hearings and careful crafting by congressional staff. The bill has been extremely well vetted and has received broad bipartisan support in the Senate. . . . Native communities cannot afford another year of the status quo when it comes to the federal response to their public safety needs.

> "The approach that the [Bureau of In-
> dian Affairs] has taken in addressing
> justice issues in tribal communities has
> demonstrated that the agency is com-
> pletely out of touch with Indian coun-
> try."

The Tribal Law and Order Act's Effectiveness Depends on Bureau of Indian Affairs Reforms

Myra Pearson

Myra Pearson has served three terms as the chairwoman of the Spirit Lake Tribe's Tribal Council in North Dakota. In the following viewpoint, Pearson details how the provisions within the Tribal Law and Order Act could potentially have a tremendously positive impact on the tribal criminal justice system, provided the Bureau of Indian Affairs (BIA) implements some greatly needed reforms and steps up its efforts to be more respectful of and in tune with the needs and views of the Native American communities it is intended to serve. Pearson recounts the many shortcomings of the BIA's criminal justice programs, which she

Myra Pearson, "Testimony of Myra Pearson, Chairwoman, Spirit Lake Tribe," United States Department of Justice Consultation on the Implementation of the Tribal Law and Order Act, October 21, 2010.

99

says have been entirely inadequate, endangering, and overburdening Native Americans. She offers specific recommendations for strengthening and improving the BIA's law enforcement system, focusing upon increasing officer population, improving officer training, increasing access to training, and improving training facilities. In addition, Pearson notes, increased funding for tribal court systems is essential to ensure that the prosecutions of criminals proceed in a timely fashion and are capable of implementing the stricter regulatory powers granted by the Tribal Law and Order Act. Finally, Pearson asserts, the Tribal Law and Order Act's requirements for greater communication between federal government agencies need to be extended to the local community level, so that agencies have plans in place that are best suited to the diverse needs of individual Native American communities.

As you read, consider the following questions:

1. Why does Pearson say that many people in the Spirit Lake community have stopped reporting criminal activity?

2. What is the percentage rate of attrition (decrease in number) of training recruits at the basic training academy in Artesia, New Mexico?

3. What opportunity does Pearson indicate would be provided by having regional training academies?

The Tribal Law and Order Act calls for federal agencies to significantly change the manner of delivery of justice services to tribal communities in a number of ways. Having reviewed the many provisions in the act I believe that the impact on tribes will vary greatly depending upon current services and resources available to the tribal justice system. I believe the Tribal Law and Order Act has the potential to either become an historical piece of legislation that will forever change the face of our tribal justice systems or it will become nothing more than a well-intentioned piece of legislation that stalls out, all of which is dependent entirely on how the act is implemented.

In my mind we are only going to see this as an historic period in the development of our tribal justice systems if we implement this legislation while being both realistic and honest in our assessment and our path for change. It is in that spirit of realism and honesty that I would like to deliver both my comments about our present justice system on the Spirit Lake reservation and what I believe to be realistic approaches that can and should be taken under the Tribal Law and Order Act to implement meaningful change.

Failures of BIA Law Enforcement

Currently the Spirit Lake Tribe receives law enforcement services through the BIA [Bureau of Indian Affairs]. The services that we receive can be characterized as inadequate at best. Our services have declined to the point that when you call law enforcement for assistance it is rare for an officer to come and assist. In the rare instances that an officer responds to a call the response is generally inadequate with little to no follow-up investigation. Add to this the fact that officers generally have no backup and a very dangerous situation has been created for the officer and the community. Additionally, what few officers we do have are oftentimes detailed to other reservations for extended periods of time, further compounding our personnel shortages. Of course I would be remiss if I did not mention the fact that investigations rarely occur unless felony activity is involved, leaving me wondering why we distinguish the BIA investigators from FBI agents, as they all seem to believe that they bear no responsibility for investigating crimes unless they are delineated in the Major Crimes Act.

That said, I believe we are truly in an era of community policing, and by that I do not mean police are leading with the assistance of the community, but rather community members are launching their own investigations into crimes. Our community has so little faith in BIA law enforcement that they are being forced to take matters into their own hands. In recent years we have seen our tribal property stolen, our community members victimized and even our courthouse burned and yet we see no accountability and little to no response on the part of law enforcement. What message are we sending that one can burn down a courthouse and there will be no accountability? The only good news in all of this is that BIA law enforcement services have gotten so bad that there is seemingly nowhere to go but up.

The issues that I see with the current law enforcement services provided by the Bureau of Indian Affairs include: officer shortages, training deficiencies and inadequate facilities.

Officer Shortages: Office shortages have plagued the tribal justice system at Spirit Lake for many years, resulting in slow response times, inadequate investigations and reports, and a number of related problems. It has gotten to the point that many people are not even reporting criminal activity as they have no faith that anything will be done to help them.

Recommendations:

1) There are several tribal colleges across the nation providing an excellent opportunity for the recruitment of prospective law enforcement officers. The BIA has done little to focus on postsecondary educational institutions to actively recruit qualified candidates to enter BIA law enforcement services. I believe that the local agencies should be engaging our youth and people who are demonstrating an interest in pursuing careers in criminal justice. A simple bi-annual visit to area community colleges should be a part of the responsibilities for active-duty law enforcement officers.

2) Additionally the placement of officers plays a big role in retention, and if efforts are made to ensure placement closer to an individual's home community that would be a signifi-

cant factor in recruitment and retention not to mention that this promotes community-oriented policing and investment in our tribal community.

3) Hiring qualified applicants in senior positions is crucial. There is little to no information made available to the tribe on the hiring process for BIA law enforcement officers. Tribes have little to no input into the candidates for such positions as police chiefs who have a significant impact on the operations of local law enforcement.

4) Providing alternative locations for completion of the basic training academy is essential. Currently the academy located in Artesia, New Mexico, is the only BIA training facility in the nation. The fact that recruits are expected to relocate for an extended period of 4 months is often a barrier to employment as many of the most qualified individuals have dependent children and family members. The isolation that these individuals experience is a factor in the 47% attrition [decrease in number] rates for the academy in Artesia, NM. One means to overcome this barrier is to regionalize BIA police academies. For example the United Tribes Technical College (hereinafter "UTTC"), which is located in Bismarck, North Dakota, provides an excellent location to serve as an academy for the entire Great Plains region. UTTC is a tribal college that is within driving distance of many tribal communities including those located in North Dakota, South Dakota, Minnesota, and Montana. The close proximity of UTTC to these tribal communities would enable weekly visits for recruits while they complete their training. This small factor would have a huge impact on the attrition rates for BIA law enforcement officers. Additionally the UTTC is a fully accredited educational institute and has offered an associate's degree in criminal justice studies for more than 30 years. The UTTC also has an existing MOU with the BIA to provide supplemental in-service training to law enforcement officers and has already outlined a plan for the delivery of training and officer placement.

Lack of Training: It is imperative that the officers who are providing law enforcement services on the Spirit Lake reservation be adequately trained both for their safety and for the safety of the community. It is alarming that BIA officers are expected to respond to often volatile crimes such as domestic violence, with little to no backup. This creates a dangerous situation not only for the officers but also for the victims on the scene.

Recommendations:

1) Mandate ongoing education as a requirement for ongoing employment to ensure the provision of quality law enforcement services to the Spirit Lake Tribe.

2) Allow BIA employees to attend national and regional training events as well as training offered through tribal community colleges in furtherance of required continuing education credits. Regional academies, such as the one proposed at UTTC, are an essential part of providing relevant training for recruits and active duty law enforcement officers. It has been clearly stated by tribes for many years that the needs of tribes and the demographics of tribes vary greatly. The development of regional academies would foster environments in which general law enforcement training could be provided, but it also provides a tremendous opportunity for issue-specific training that is relevant to tribes in the region. The training academy should focus on basic training for new officers and should also include continuing education for existing officers. Continuing education should be available regardless of an officer's desire to change their rank or position within the BIA.

Inadequate Facilities: BIA law enforcement field offices are located in buildings that are in desperate need of repair, remodel, or new construction. Attempts by the tribe to secure construction dollars has either been unsuccessful due to lack of available funding or alternatively the BIA facilities management program has authorized funds to renovate existing facilities in lieu of new construction dollars or sufficient funds to properly renovate existing facilities. The end result is that the funds came to the tribe to renovate, however, the strings attached to these funds resulted in a cosmetic face-lift but did little to enable the tribe to update the facility in a manner that would actually meet the needs of the community.

Recommendations:

1) Provide a more cohesive means for tribes to access bricks and mortar funds for facility construction whilst also addressing plans for facility operations. Rather than requiring tribes to seek construction dollars from one agency and operations funds from another, perhaps a joint process should be employed to ensure that tribes are working with necessary federal agencies from the onset of the planning process through completion of the construction and implementation phases. This is the type of process that will not only result in a building but will result in a building that facilitates the provision of services to the community.

[Among] the predominant threads that run through most of the problems that exist with facilities, recruitment, retention, hiring and training are lack of adequate funding and lack of strategic planning. Federal appropriations must be made to ensure that necessary funds are available to implement provisions of the Tribal Law and Order Act. Strategic planning should be a part of the process for each field agency and area office and such planning should involve input from the tribes so that we have meaningful input into the improvement of justice services in our respective communities.

Crucial Funding Needed for Tribal Courts and Prosecution

The Tribal Law and Order Act also includes many provisions that will significantly impact tribal and federal prosecutions. Whether looking at the sentencing enhancements, communications across agency and jurisdictional lines or the access to crime data, the fact remains that all of these efforts will require additional funds. In particular I would like to reference the significant shortfalls in the ... contract dollars that are provided to the Spirit Lake Tribe for the operations of our court system. The ... contract dollars are not sufficient to provide for even the most basic justice system personnel, which in and of itself is contrary to existing federal law. The Spirit Lake Tribe is only able to support a judge and a few members of the administrative staff from our current ... court budget. All other funding for the court is provided either through local EDF dollars or comes from competitive grant programs through the Department of Justice. It is unbelievable that we are required to rely on competitive grants to provide such basic services as an associate judge, a data entry clerk, or a probation officer. To this end it is time that the budget for the BIA be reevaluated in terms of the funds that are funneling from the top down through the area offices. Perhaps by cutting out some of the middlemen we can save enough dollars to actually provide adequate ... contract funding to our tribal courts, thereby allowing additional enhancement services and programs to be funded through competitive grants, as is the case for the other courts in this nation.

In terms of the Tribal Law and Order Act this fact is even more significant as the provisions of the act are clear that only those tribal courts that are providing basic services such as defense counsel will be entitled to apply increased sentencing options.

Communication, Collaboration and Data

One of the predominant aspects of the Tribal Law and Order Act is the call for information sharing with respect to investigations, prosecutions and crime data as a whole. I agree that such efforts are necessary, however as the Tribal Law and Order Act is implemented, it is imperative that the efforts to coordinate services include input from the local level. It does a disservice to our communities to have policies, procedures and plans developed in an office in [Washington] D.C. by people who have no clue what our tribal infrastructures or demographics are. We need consultation not only at national sessions such as this, but more importantly we need consultation at the local level through strategic planning committees who would meet to more specifically outline a plan of action for each tribal community. Through the development of a Tribal Law and Order Act implementation plan each tribe would have direct input into addressing their needs and would further be fully informed as to what measures federal agencies are taking with respect to their tribal community. Another benefit to such a process would be that the tribe would be able to identify areas that are within the tribe's control and could be developed to increase the positive impact of the act. We are continuously saying and hearing that a one-size-fits-all approach does not work in Indian country, so in true government-to-government fashion let's change that approach to one that is more individualized and to one that involves less bureaucratic input and more grassroots input from the people who are in the field doing the work.

Fundamental Changes and Greater Accountability Are Needed

In closing, it is my opinion the approach that the BIA has taken in addressing justice issues in tribal communities has demonstrated that the agency is completely out of touch with Indian country. There have been far too many people climbing the ranks and leaving the field offices ill equipped to meet the needs of the communities they are supposed to be serving. I think it is time for the United States Congress to take a hard look at the upper-level administration within the Bureau of Indian Affairs and assess what needs to improve within the leadership of the BIA. A team will only be as good as its leader and from what the BIA is showing us, leadership is poorly lacking. As tribal leaders we are developing short- and long-term strategic plans to develop our communities, to justify our requests for federal funding and to further support our expenditures of those funds. That same process should be mandated of the BIA with respect to the programs and funds that are administered through their agency. This would provide a measure of accountability to both the United States Congress and the tribes that the BIA is supposed to be serving and would be a step toward real and honest change.

Periodical and Internet Sources Bibliography

The following articles have been selected to supplement the diverse views presented in this chapter.

Carol Berry	"Native Civil Rights Explored," Indian Country Today Media Network, August 16, 2011. http://indiancountrytodaymedianetwork.com.
Peter d'Errico	"'Special Rights' Is a Loaded Term," Indian Country Today Media Network, August 29, 2011. http://indiancountrytodaymedianetwork.com.
Troy A. Eid	"The Tribal Law and Order Act: An 'Aggressive Fight' Worth Winning," *Federal Lawyer*, March/April, 2010.
Sarah Garrett	"Cherokee Freedmen Deserve the Benefits of Citizenship," *Oklahoma Daily*, August 29, 2011.
Jefferson Keel	"Don't Be Played the Fool; It's About Sovereignty," Indian Country Today Media Network, April 1, 2011. http://indiancountrytodaymedianetwork.com.
Matt Rosenberg	"Audit: Bureau of Indian Affairs Jails Still Mismanaged," Social Capital Review, May 26, 2011. http://socialcapitalreview.org.
Robert O. Saunooke	"Tribal Justice: The Case for Strengthening Inherent Sovereignty," American Bar Association, October 2008. http://apps.americanbar.org.
Paul Schmelzer	"Bachmann Votes Against Act to Help Native American Police Combat Rape 'Epidemic,'" *Minnesota Independent*, July 28, 2010.

Chapter 3

How Do Disputes over Resources and Artifacts Affect Native Americans?

Chapter Preface

While some Native American tribes are enthusiastic to embrace the economic opportunities afforded by renewable energy development, other tribes are battling in court to prevent large solar development projects on the grounds that they will destroy sites that are sacred to them. In California, the Quechan tribe filed a lawsuit against the Bureau of Land Management (BLM) to delay the start of the Imperial Valley solar project, slated for development near El Centro, California, on nearly sixty-five hundred acres of land that are owned by the BLM. In the lawsuit, the Quechan tribe asserts that the BLM violated several federal statutes governing the use of land that has cultural significance to Native Americans. The tribe argues that neither the BLM nor the Department of the Interior adequately evaluated the "public lands that are the subject of the Imperial Valley ROD are within the traditional territory of the Quechan Indian Tribe and contain cultural and biological resources of significance to the Tribe, its government, and its members."[1] The tribe was granted an injunction that halted the development on December 15, 2010, by a US District Court judge who said that "Native Americans are entitled to 'special consideration' when an agency is fulfilling its consultation requirements for development of land under NHPA's [National Historic Preservation Act's] consultation process."[2] Among other concerns, the tribe objected to the dangers presented to an animal that is central to their creation mythology, the flat-tailed horned lizard, and the building of solar dishes on the cremated remains of tribal ancestors.

Because of substantial grant monies offered to green energy developers as part of the American Recovery and Reinvestment Act of 2009, several projects in California were rushed through the approval process so that they could qualify before the offer expired at the end of 2010. The majority of these projects met with opposition from area tribes. In December 2010, La Cuna de Aztlán Sacred Sites Protection Circle, along with other environmental groups, filed a federal lawsuit to block six large-scale solar projects planned in the California deserts. The group's complaint asserted that they had expressed concerns that the projects would destroy ancient geoglyphs (large-scale images created using various means, such as removing vegetation and exposing underlying soil), grave sites, and artifacts early on during the approval process and they were ignored. In a document compiled by the La Cuna de Aztlán Sacred Sites Protection Circle, they state: "A giant geoglyph of the Kokopelli, the indigenous hunchback icon with a flute, lies within the right of way acreage of the proposed Blythe solar project eight miles east of Blythe, California. BLM officials have visited the site of the Kokopelli, yet they continue to sign off on the paperwork in pursuit of the implementation of the proposed solar power plants. This document was sent out in search of assistance in protecting the Kokopelli and over 25 other indigenous sacred sites that are exposed to destruction by off-road vehicles and now, mega-solar power plants."[3]

Native American opposition to large solar projects is just one example of disputes between Native Americans and non–Native Americans over natural resources and protecting sacred sites. The viewpoints in this chapter focus on various disputes over natural resources and legislation to regulate the handling of archaeologically significant Native American objects and human remains. The authors cover such subjects as the Native American Graves Protection and Repatriation Act; northeastern Arizona water rights settlement; the development of Glen Cove in Vallejo, California; and Native American investment in renewable energy.

Notes

1. "Complaint of Quechan Indian Tribe for Declaratory and Injunctive Relief," United States District Court for the Southern District of California, October 29, 2010.
2. Daniel Firger, "Native Americans Challenge Solar Projects on Federal and Tribal Lands," *Climate Law Blog*, Center for Climate Change Law, Columbia University, March 14, 2011. http://blogs.law.columbia.edu/climatechange.
3. Alfredo Acosta Figueroa, "Stop the Destruction of Our Sacred Sites," La Cuna de Aztlán Sacred Sites Protection Circle, 2010, p. 1.

"Hundreds of thousands of objects of Indian art, cultural property, and human
remains have been returned to their
lineal descendants or culturally affiliated tribes. . . . This is a tremendous
accomplishment whose importance cannot be understated."

The Native American Graves Protection and Repatriation Act at Twenty: Reaching the Limits of Our National Consensus

Steven J. Gunn

Steven J. Gunn is adjunct professor of law at the Washington University School of Law and an attorney in St. Louis, Missouri. In the following viewpoint, Gunn emphasizes the successes that the Native American Graves Protection and Repatriation Act (NAGPRA) has had in restoring human remains and objects of cultural, historical, and spiritual significance to Native Americans since 1990, when it was implemented. Gunn outlines the

Steven J. Gunn, "The Native American Graves Protection and Repatriation Act at Twenty: Reaching the Limits of Our National Consensus," *William Mitchell Law Review,* vol. 36, January 18, 2010, pp. 503–512, 531–532. Reproduced by permission of the author.

provisions of the act and provides historical and cultural context for the creation of NAGPRA by describing how Native American remains and artifacts were viewed and handled prior to the act and by relating the role that remains and artifacts play in various Native American spiritual and cultural traditions. Gunn declares that there is widespread agreement among Americans and national agencies that Native Americans should have the authority to decide what to do with their ancestors' human remains and artifacts, but he admits that there are difficult questions of ownership that remain unanswered by NAGPRA when the origins of remains and artifacts are unclear or disputed.

As you read, consider the following questions:

1. According to Janine Pease Windy Boy, why are medicine bundles so important to Native American society?

2. According to the viewpoint, by the late 1980s the remains of how many Native Americans were held in museums, agencies, universities, historical societies, and other institutions?

3. How many millions of dollars worth of Native American artifacts were sold in Arizona in 1982, according to the viewpoint?

The Native American Graves Protection and Repatriation Act (NAGPRA), enacted on November 16, 1990,[1] provides far-reaching protections for the sacred objects, cultural patrimony [heritage], funerary objects, and ancestral human remains of American Indians and Indian tribes. With few exceptions, the act requires federally funded museums and federal agencies to repatriate [give back] to Indians and Indian tribes any such items in their possession or control.[2] Among these

1. American Graves Protection and Repatriation Act, Pub. L. No. 101-601, 104 Stat. 3048 (1990) (codified as amended at 25 U.S.C. §§ 3001-3013 (2006), 18 U.S.C. § 1170 (2006)).

2. 25 U.S.C. § 3005 (2006).

items[3] are works of great artistic and cultural value, including the thousand-year-old "exquisite black-on-white pottery" of the Mimbres people, "decorated with ingenious animal and human motifs;"[4] the wampum belts of the Iroquois, on which the tribes of the confederacy recorded major historical events, treaties, and laws;[5] and the spectacular headdresses of the plains Indians, made of buckskin and eagle feathers, buffalo fur and horns, among other materials. U.S. Senator Pete Domenici aptly described these and other items at the time of NAGPRA's passage: "They are more than just interesting artifacts; they are works of art."[6]

Many, if not most, of these items were stolen or seized from Indians during the last two centuries. They were looted from Indian villages, ceremonial grounds, massacre sites, battlefields, schools, and prisons; excavated from burial grounds and unmarked Indian graves; and otherwise misappropriated from Indians and their tribes.[7]

In addition to requiring the repatriation of native cultural items held by museums and agencies, NAGPRA prohibits the unauthorized excavation and removal of Indian artifacts, cultural property, and remains from federal or tribal lands;[8] safe-

3. The terms "artifacts," "cultural property," and "Indian art" are used interchangeably in this paper. They are meant to refer to the cultural items listed in NAGPRA, with the exception of human remains. See 25 U.S.C. § 3001(3) (2006). These items include sacred objects, cultural patrimony, and funerary objects. Id. For definitions, see infra notes 60-68 and accompanying text.

4. Andrew Gulliford, *Sacred Objects and Sacred Places: Preserving Tribal Traditions* 45 (2000).

5. Martin Sullivan, A Museum Perspective on Repatriation: Issues and Opportunities, 24 Ariz. St. L.J. 283, 285-86 (1992).

6. U.S. Sen. Pete Domenici (R-NM), Preface B to *Protecting the Past* v (George S. Smith & John E. Ehrenhard eds., 1991) (emphasis added).

7. Suzan Shown Harjo, Introduction to *Mending the Circle: A Native American Repatriation Guide* 3, 4-6 (Barbara Meister ed., 1995). Introduction available at http://www.repatriationfoundation.org/pdf/mending%20the% 20circle/CoverBeginning.pdf. See also infra notes 35-52 and accompanying text (discussing the misappropriation of American Indian artifacts and remains).

8. 25 U.S.C. § 3002 (2006).

guards tribal ownership rights to any such property or remains discovered on federal or tribal lands;[9] and prohibits trafficking in Indian artifacts and remains obtained in violation of the act.[10]

Widespread Support for NAGPRA

NAGPRA was the product of a national consensus concerning the dignity and respect due American Indians, their property, and their cultures.[11] This consensus affirmed that, whenever possible, objects of great religious or cultural importance to tribes ought to be returned to the tribes for contemporary ceremonial and cultural use, not held in museum collections.[12] It also affirmed that American Indians ought to be able to bury the remains of their ancestors in a respectful and culturally appropriate manner.[13] Support for NAGPRA was widespread and included the endorsements of numerous major associations of museums, scientists, historical societies, and Indian tribes.[14]

Rennard Strickland, a legal historian of Osage and Cherokee heritage, describes NAGPRA's significance:

> The act is important because it represents the new American consensus about sacred objects and cultural patrimony, a consensus not only of members of the Congress and of Native peoples, but also of very diverse groups of scientists, museum trustees, and art collectors. That consensus is: The

9. Id.
10. 25 U.S.C. § 3001(13) (2006); 18 U.S.C. § 1170(a) (2006).
11. See C. Timothy McKeown & Sherry Hutt, In the Smaller Scope of Conscience: The Native American Graves Protection and Repatriation Act Twelve Years After, 21 UCLA J. Envtl. L. & Pol'y 153, 154-56 (2002).
12. See id. at 153-57.
13. See id. at 155-56.
14. Among the Act's supporters were the American Association of Museums, Society for American Archaeology, Society for Historical Archaeology, Society of Professional Archaeologists, Archaeological Institute of America, American Anthropological Association, American Association of Physical Anthropologists, National Conference of State Historic Preservation Officers, National Trust for Historic Preservation, Preservation Action, Association on American Indian Affairs, Native American Rights Fund, and National Congress of American Indians. Id. at 154.

sacred culture of Native Americans and Native Hawaiians is a living heritage. This culture is a vital part of the ongoing lifeways of the United States, and as such, must be respected, protected, and treated as a living spiritual entity—not as a remnant museum specimen.[15]

Many Indians consider sacred objects, cultural patrimony, and funerary objects to be vital to their survival as a people. Sacred objects, such as medicine bags and bundles, "possess life forces of their own."[16] They are the "prime backbone" for many tribes, helping assure their members that they will retain their Indian identities, cultures, and religions for generations to come.[17] According to Janine Pease Windy Boy, president of Little Big Horn College and a Crow Indian:

> There are some ceremonies that cannot happen unless certain medicine bundles are present and their power and personage is part of the community that undertakes the ceremony. . . . Now if the bundle is gone, then the function of that society is broken and the value that society brought, the relationships that it made among the people, the songs, the stories, the history, the cohesiveness of that group of people, the family nature of that society is broken, and that is a human tragedy.[18]

Other items, like the Yei B'Chei or ceremonial dance masks of the Navajo Nation, are considered "living gods."[19] The Yei B'Chei represent the "'heartbeat' of the Navajo people" and are referred to by tribal members not as masks, but as "gods."[20] They are the property of the entire community and cannot be bought or sold by any individual.[21]

---

15. Rennard Strickland, *Tonto's Revenge: Reflections on American Indian Culture and Policy* 85-86 (1997).
16. Gulliford, supra note 4, at 42.
17. Id. at 56.
18. Id. at 65-66 (quoting Janine Pease Windy Boy).
19. *United States v. Corrow*, 119 F.3d 796, 798 (10th Cir. 1997).
20. Jori Finkel, Is Everything Sacred?: A Respected Art Dealer is Busted for Selling a Cheyenne War Bonnet, Legal Affairs, July/Aug. 2003, at 65, 66.
21. Gulliford, supra note 4, at 64-65.

Despite the great importance of these items to Indian people, their aesthetic qualities and historic value have created great demand among non-Indian collectors and museums. Single pieces of Mimbres pottery have sold for up to $75,000;[22] collections of Navajo Yei B'Chei have drawn $70,000;[23] and, in one case, an assortment of Tlingit ceremonial objects was valued at $250,000.[24] It has been reported that "annual sales of Native American art at the auction houses of Christie's and Sotheby's peaked at $10 million in 1998."[25]

There Have Been Many Successes, but Challenges Remain

In its first twenty years, NAGPRA has seen the return of hundreds of thousands of sacred objects, objects of cultural patrimony, and funerary objects to Indians and Indian tribes.[26] It has also seen the return of tens of thousands of human remains.[27] The act has placed Indians in control of these items.[28] It has led, more often than not, to greater communication and collaboration between museums, scientists, and American Indians, and to a heightened respect for the sanctity of Indian art, cultural property, and human remains.

Despite these successes, persistent challenges remain. While hundreds of thousands of objects of Indian art and cultural property have been affiliated with, and repatriated to, present-day tribes, even more remain unidentified, languishing in the custody of museums and government agencies. These items have been classified as Native American, within the meaning of NAGPRA, but gaps in the evidentiary record so far have prevented their cultural affiliation with one or more present-day tribes. The costs—to tribes, museums, and government

22. Id. at 47.
23. *United States v. Corrow*, 119 F.3d at 799.
24. *Johnson v. Chilkat Indian Vill.*, 457 F. Supp. 384, 386 n.1 (D. Alaska 1978).
25. Finkel, supra note 20.
26. See infra note 121 and accompanying text.
27. See id.
28. See infra note 130 and accompanying text.

agencies—of establishing such affiliations can be exorbitant. Still other items, like the skeletal remains of the 9,000-year-old "Ancient One" known as Kennewick Man, are so old that their mere identification as Native American, not to mention their cultural affiliation with a particular tribe, has been contested.[29]

The challenges posed by unaffiliated and ancient items lie beyond the boundaries of the national consensus described by Strickland.[30] Who should bear the extraordinary costs of establishing the cultural affiliation of presently unaffiliated items held by museums and federal agencies? How much are we willing to spend to ensure—or attempt to ensure—that Indian artifacts, cultural property, and human remains are returned to their rightful owners? To what extent—and to whom—should museums and federal agencies be required to repatriate items that cannot be affiliated with any given tribe?

What disposition should be required—or permitted—for newly discovered artifacts and remains so ancient that they bear no readily apparent affiliation with present-day Indians, let alone a particular tribe? How should the interests of museum curators and scientists in the display and study of these ancient objects and remains be balanced against the interests of Indians seeking their speedy return?

There are no easy answers to these questions—not in NAGPRA and not in our national consciousness. . . .

What Prompted the Need for NAGPRA

NAGPRA was prompted, in large part, by revelations in the late 1980s that federally funded museums and government agencies were in possession of millions of objects of Indian art, cultural property, and human remains, and that most of these objects and remains had been "stolen or improperly acquired."[35]

29. *Bonnichsen v. United States*, 367 F.3d 864 (9th Cir. 2004).
30. See Strickland, supra note 15.
35. Jack F. Trope & Walter R. Echo-Hawk, The Native American Graves Protection and Repatriation Act: Background and Legislative History, 24 Ariz. St. L.J. 35, 44-45 (1992). See also id. at 39-43.

The most staggering revelations concerned Indian human remains. In February 1987, the Smithsonian Institution reported to Congress that its collection contained the remains of 18,584 American Indians.[36] This disclosure was shocking, but it did not begin to capture the full extent to which the human remains of American Indians had been acquired by non-Indians. Conservative estimates suggest that, by the late 1980s, the remains of some 200,000 American Indians and Alaska Natives were held in museums, agencies, universities, historical societies, and other institutions in the United States and around the world.[37] Among the remains were severed skulls, brains, bones, and other body parts.

Much has been written about the factors contributing to this extraordinary accumulation of Indian remains in non-Indian institutions.[38] Several such factors are worthy of brief mention here. First, in the mid-nineteenth century, leading American anthropologists began collecting and studying Indian skulls, intending to establish through cranial measurements the racial inferiority of Indians to whites.[39] Not long

---

36. S. Rep. No. 101-473, at 2 (1990), available at http:// rla.unc.edu/saa/repat/Legislative/ lgm002.html. This figure includes 14,523 sets of remains from North American Indians and 4,061 Eskimo, Aleut, and Koniag remains. Id. Historian Andrew Gulliford notes that "although native peoples represent less than 1 percent of today's American population and were an equally small demographic percentage a century ago, [in 1987] they represented 54.4 percent of the Smithsonian's collection of 34,000 human specimens." Gulliford, supra note 4, at 22.

37. Michael F. Brown & Margaret M. Bruchac, NAGPRA from the Middle Distance: Legal Puzzles and Unintended Consequences, in *Imperialism, Art and Restitution* 193, 196 (John Henry Merryman ed., 2006); David J. Harris, Respect for the Living and Respect for the Dead: Return of Indian and Other Native American Burial Remains, 39 Wash. U. J. Urb. & Contemp. L. 195, 195 n.3 (1991).

38. E.g., Kathleen S. Fine-Dare, *Grave Injustice: The American Indian Repatriation Movement and NAGPRA* (Gerald Sider & Kirk Dombrowski eds., University of Nebraska Press 2002); David Hurst Thomas, Skull Wars: Kennewick Man, Archaeology, and the Battle for the American Identity (2000); Gulliford, supra note 4; Robert E. Bieder, *A Brief Historical Survey of the Exploration of American Indian Remains* (1990), reprinted in Hearings on S. 1021 and S. 1980 Before the Senate Select Comm. on Indian Affairs, 101st Cong., 2d Sess. 278-363 (May 14, 1990).

39. Robert E. Bieder, *Science Encounters the Indian, 1820-1880* (1986).

thereafter, in 1868, the U.S. surgeon general made the collection and study of Indian remains official federal policy, directing U.S. Army personnel to collect Indian remains for the Army Medical Museum. As a result of this policy, thousands of Indian skulls and other body parts "began making their way from the battlefields of the West into medical collections of the U.S. Army and eventually into the physical anthropological collections of museums."[40] Second, under the [American] Antiquities Act of 1906,[41] and later the Archaeological Resources Protection Act of 1979,[42] Indian remains located on federal lands were classified as federal property and treated as "objects of antiquity" or "archaeological resources." Federal agencies had broad authority to permit the excavation and removal of these remains, provided that "the examinations, excavations, and gatherings are undertaken for the benefit of reputable museums, universities, colleges, or other recognized scientific or educational institutions, with a view to increasing the knowledge of such objects, and that the gatherings shall be made for permanent preservation in public museums."[43] Finally, competition among America's museums for Indian remains was intense, leading to the widespread—and often rapacious—collection of Indian skeletons.

Indian skeletons were not the only items coveted by collectors and museums. W. Richard West, Jr., director of the National Museum of the American Indian and a Southern Cheyenne Indian, reports that by the early twentieth century, millions of Indian cultural objects had been acquired by public and private museums:

> Large amounts of native cultural patrimony, often viewed as
> the last physical vestiges of dead or dying cultures and

40. W. Richard West, Jr., Repatriation, in *Encyclopedia of North American Indians: Native American History, Culture, and Life from Paleo-Indians to the Present* 543, 544 (Frederick E. Hoxie ed., 1996).

41. Act of June 8, 1906, ch. 3060, 34 Stat. 225 (codified at 16 U.S.C. §§ 431-433).

42. Pub. L. No. 96-95, 93 Stat. 722 (1979) (codified at 16 U.S.C. § 470aa-mm).

43. 16 U.S.C § 432 (2006).

peoples, began moving into museums through means fair and foul—some of it sold by native people to collectors and much else literally stolen. . . . Thus, by the early twentieth century several large public and private museums, including the Smithsonian Institution's National Museum of Natural History, New York's Heye Foundation Museum of the American Indian and American Museum of Natural History, and the Field Museum in Chicago held collections of native objects that, cumulatively, numbered in the millions.[44]

In a report to Congress in August 1979, the U.S. Department of the Interior described the nature and extent of the problem:

Museum records show that some sacred objects were sold by their original Native owner or owners. In many instances, however, the chain of title does not lead to the original owners. Some religious property left the original ownership during military confrontations, was included in the spoils of war and eventually fell to the control of museums. Also in times past, sacred objects were lost by Native owners as a result of less violent pressures exerted by federally sponsored missionaries and Indian agents.

. . .

Most sacred objects were stolen from their original owners. In other cases, religious property was converted and sold by Native people who did not have ownership or title to the sacred object.

. . .

Today in many parts of the country, it is common for "pothunters" to enter Indian and public lands for the purpose of illegally expropriating sacred objects. Interstate traf-

44. West, supra note 40, at 544. For a description of the race to collect Indian artifacts in the Northwest, see Douglas Cole, *Captured Heritage: The Scramble for Northwest Coast Artifacts* (1985).

ficking in and exporting of such property flourishes, with some of these sacred objects eventually entering into the possession of museums.[45]

Laws Prior to NAGPRA Were Insufficient

In December 1987, the U.S. General Accounting Office reported that nearly 44,000 of the 136,000 archaeological sites in the Four Corners states of Arizona, Colorado, New Mexico, and Utah had experienced looting of Indian artifacts and cultural property.[46] Many of the items stolen from these sites commanded high prices on the black market, including, as noted above, $60,000 to $70,000 for a single piece of Mimbres pottery.[47] In Arizona alone, it was determined that, in 1982, "$2.7 million in artifacts were sold . . . 95% of which had been removed from federal lands."[48] It was also estimated that another $9 million in damage had been done to archaeological sites and cultural artifacts in Arizona in 1982.[49] These figures were consistent with estimates for the rest of the country.[50]

Existing laws proved inadequate to protect against the theft of Indian artifacts and human remains or to ensure the repatriation of items already seized. For example, while numerous states had laws barring the excavation or disturbance of remains and funerary objects in unmarked graves,[51] these laws were under-enforced. Moreover, less than a handful of

45. Trope & Echo-Hawk, supra note 35, at 44 (quoting Sec'y of Interior, Fed. Agencies Task Force, American Indian Religious Freedom Act Report 77 (1979)).
46. U.S. Gen. Accounting Office, *Cultural Resources: Problems Protecting and Preserving Federal Archeological Resources* No. RCED-88-3, 22 (1987) [hereinafter G.A.O.]. See also H. Comm. on Interior & Insular Affairs, *The Destruction of America's Archaeological Heritage: Looting and Vandalism of Indian Archaeological Sites in the Four Corners States of the Southwest* (Comm. Print No. 6 1988).
47. G.A.O., supra note 46, at 29.
48. Id. at 101.
49. Id.
50. George S. Smith & John E. Ehrenhard, Introduction to *Protecting the Past*, supra note 6.

Repatriated Objects and Human Remains

How many Native American human remains and cultural items have been repatriated since the passage of NAGPRA?

There is no single source for this information. While museums and federal agencies are required to keep their own record of repatriations, NAGPRA does not require museums and federal agencies to report repatriations to the secretary of the interior or to the National Park Service. Museums and federal agencies are required, however, to publish notices in the *Federal Register* when they have determined that Native American human remains, funerary objects, sacred objects, and/or objects of cultural patrimony are culturally affiliated and are eligible for repatriation. The national NAGPRA program compiles statistics twice yearly on the total number of Native American human remains, funerary objects, sacred objects, and objects of cultural significance for which *Federal Register* notices have been published. The current statistics (updated on September 30, 2009) are as follows—

Human remains: 38,671 individuals

Associated funerary objects: 998,731 (includes many small items, such as beads)

Unassociated funerary objects: 144,163 (includes many small items, such as beads)

Sacred objects: 4,303

Objects of cultural patrimony: 948

Objects that are both sacred and patrimonial: 822

National Park Service, US Department of the Interior, "National NAGPRA: Frequently Asked Questions," 2009. www.nps.gov.

states had laws requiring the repatriation of cultural property or remains already excavated or otherwise unlawfully acquired.[52]

State repatriation laws were passed in response to public displays of Indian artifacts and human remains and mass excavations of Indian burial grounds in the years immediately preceding NAGPRA's adoption. For example, "[i]n 1989, Hawaii appropriated $5 million from its land banking law to purchase a Native Hawaiian burial ground owned by a private developer who had dug up over 900 remains in order to build a hotel—$500,000 of those funds were used to rebury the dead."[53] Similarly, in 1989, Kansas passed legislation closing the "Indian Burial Pit" near Salina, Kansas, which had publicly displayed the remains and associated funerary objects of 165 Indians.[54] The Kansas State Historical Society later repatriated the Indian remains in its collection.[55]

These highly publicized events, and others like them, led to a national awareness of the historic and ongoing misappropriation of Indian art, cultural property, and human remains and, in turn, to a national consensus that these items ought to be returned to their rightful owners. This consensus was the driving force behind Congress's enactment of NAGPRA in 1990. . . .

51. Trope and Echo-Hawk report that, as of 1992, thirty-four states had passed laws protecting unmarked burial sites. Trope & Echo-Hawk, supra note 35, at 52 n.79. They note that "[t]hese laws typically prohibit intentional disturbance of unmarked graves, provide guidelines to protect the graves, and mandate disposition of human remains from the graves in a way that guarantees reburial after a study period." Id. at 52.

52. Arizona, Hawaii, Kansas, and Nebraska had enacted repatriation laws prior to NAGPRA's adoption. Id. at 53-54. California adopted similar legislation in 1991. Id. at 54.

53. Id. at 53.

54. See id. See also Gulliford, supra note 4, at 22.

55. See Trope & Echo Hawk, supra note 35, at 53. During this period, many museums and universities voluntarily repatriated their collections of Indian artifacts and remains. See Gulliford, supra note 4, at 24.

Challenges to NAGPRA Should Be Solved by Compromise

When Congress enacted NAGPRA in 1990, it responded to a national consensus that present-day Indian tribes—not government agencies, museums, or collectors—should be the keepers of their sacred cultural objects and ancestral remains. Since 1990, hundreds of thousands of objects of Indian art, cultural property, and human remains have been returned to their lineal descendants or culturally affiliated tribes under NAGPRA. This is a tremendous accomplishment whose importance cannot be understated. Yet difficult challenges remain for which there is no national consensus. In the case of ancient, unidentified cultural items, the interests of scientists eager to study them crash headlong into those of Indians who claim them as their own and seek their immediate return. Categorical solutions favoring one side over the other are unlikely. Instead, compromises will be required of scientists and Indians alike, and those compromises will be facilitated only by mutual understanding and respect for the interests on all sides.

Notes Referred to in Notes

60. 25 U.S.C. § 3001(3)(C) (2006).

61. 43 C.F.R. § 10.2(d)(3) (2008). The House Report on NAGPRA made clear that "the definition of 'sacred objects' is intended to include both objects needed for ceremonies currently practiced by traditional Native American religious practi-tioners and objects needed to renew ceremonies that are part of traditional religions." H.R. Rep. No. 101-877, at 17 (1990).

62. 25 U.S.C. § 3001(3)(D). Cultural patrimony and sacred objects are not mutually exclusive categories. In fact, many items repatriated under NAGPRA have been classified both as objects of cultural patrimony and sacred objects.

63. 43 C.F.R. § 10.2(d)(4).

64. Gulliford, supra note 4, at 43.

65. Id. at 44.

66. Robert A. Williams, Jr., *Linking Arms Together: American Indian Treaty Visions of Law and Peace, 1600-1800* 51-52 (1997).

67. 25 U.S.C. § 3001(3)(A).

68. Id. § 3001(3)(B).

121. National NAGPRA Frequently Asked Questions, http://www.cr.nps.gov/nagpra/FAQ/INDEX.HTM (last visited Nov. 14, 2009).

130. For an extensive list of tribal museums and cultural centers, see Gulliford, supra note 4, at app. B. For a discussion of tribal repatriation programs, see Dean B. Suagee, Building a Tribal Repatriation Program: Options for Exercising Sove-reignty, in *Mending the Circle: A Native American Repatriation Guide*, supra note 7, at 29-44.

"The right to discover the knowledge of the first Americans that may be gleaned from ancient remains belongs to the public as a whole."

The Native American Graves Protection and Repatriation Act Impedes Progress and Cooperation

Bryan W. Wolford

Bryan W. Wolford is an attorney in California, Missouri. In the following viewpoint, Wolford declares that the Native American Graves Protection and Repatriation Act (NAGPRA) presents unfair and unnecessary obstacles to scientific research, citing several cases in which ancient human remains were ordered to be turned over to tribes for burial when there was no solid connection between them. Wolford contends that it has been possible—by bypassing NAGPRA—for scientists to work closely with tribes to ensure that they are able to conduct the testing and investigation they need with human remains before they are turned over to tribes for burial. The author suggests that the US Ninth Circuit Court's ruling in one such case further complicated matters, be-

Bryan W. Wolford, *Selected Works of Bryan W. Wolford*, California, MO: ExpressO, 2010. Reproduced by permission of the author.

cause the court mistakenly interpreted NAGPRA and caused Native American remains to be identified as non–Native American, and he recommends that Congress pass amendments to NAGPRA to clearly define what remains should be designated "Native American," specify what should be done with ancient remains, and establish guidelines to allow timelines for scientific study before remains are turned over to Native Americans for burial.

As you read, consider the following questions:

1. According to Wolford, how old were the human remains discovered near Buhl, Idaho, that were given to the Shoshone-Bannock tribe?

2. What are corprolites, according to the viewpoint?

3. What cutoff date for the origin of human remains does Wolford suggest should be used to determine whether they should be classified as Native American?

Congress chiseled yet another watershed moment upon the tablet of Native American history in 1990 through the passage of the Native American Graves Protection and Repatriation Act (NAGPRA) which is heralded as an historic and landmark act and "one of the most significant pieces of human rights legislation since the Bill of Rights." Congress enacted NAGPRA to "establish rights of Indian tribes, Native Hawaiian organizations, and their lineal descendants" to the repatriation [giving back] of "certain Native American human remains, funerary objects, sacred objects, or objects of cultural patrimony [heritage] with which they are affiliated." NAGPRA further prohibits the unauthorized excavation and removal of such remains and objects from federal or tribal land and forbids the trafficking of any remains or items obtained in violation of NAGPRA. . . .

NAGPRA Coverage

NAGPRA consists of two prongs aimed at "resolv[ing] years of debate between tribes, archaeologists, and museums." The first prong establishes a procedure for the repatriation of Native American human remains and cultural property to affiliated tribes from federally funded agencies and museums. The repatriation prong provides an inventory procedure for federally funded agencies and museums possessing or controlling Native American human remains and cultural property whereby Native American tribes may request the repatriation of specific items and allows the tribes to pursue civil remedies against organizations and museums that fail to comply.

NAGPRA's second prong protects Native American cultural resources, archaeological sites, and burials from impermissible excavations and looting. This prong also requires parties to obtain a permit pursuant to the Archaeological Resources Protection Act of 1979 (ARPA) prior to the excavation of archaeological sites on federal and tribal land. Though not a complete remedial scheme, NAGPRA contains a provision against the trafficking of human remains and cultural property obtained in violation of itself. Described as the teeth of NAGPRA, 18 U.S.C. § 1170 imposes a fine or imprisonment for less than one year or both for the first offense and imprisonment for up to five years for each subsequent offense. . . .

Future Application of NAGPRA to the Study of the First Americans

Archaeologists agree that very little evidence exists regarding America's earliest inhabitants. Because the archaeological sites of the first Americans to migrate from Beringia [ancient land bridge that once joined Alaska and Siberia] remain undiscovered—and some would argue, undiscoverable due to the sea level—the best source for archaeological information about these ancient immigrants is the physical remains of Paleo-

Indians [first inhabitants of the American continent]. Even "a single ancient human hair subjected to DNA testing can reveal volumes about its owner." Unfortunately, bones preserve better than hair, and the scientists claim "legitimate educational, historical, and scientific interests" in the unhindered study of ancient skeletal remains.

Professional archaeologists recognize the importance of repatriating culturally identifiable remains to Native Americans, but they argue that culturally unaffiliated remains "should not be treated the same way as those that are more recent and unquestionably Indian." In their view, Native Americans "have no right to human remains that are so old that claims to them have to be taken on religious faith." The right to discover the knowledge of the first Americans that may be gleaned from ancient remains belongs to the public as a whole. "Respect for Native Americans should not cause us to abandon science in favor of politically expedient compromises."

Archaeologists point to the repatriation and reburial of the 10,600-year-old remains of a female discovered near Buhl, Idaho, to the Shoshone-Bannock tribe. The tribe had only inhabited the area surrounding Buhl for no more than 2,000 years, and had "only a tenuous, if any, cultural or other connection" with the remains. Nevertheless, the well-preserved skeleton was returned to the earth without any substantial scientific study or DNA analysis. The reburial of the Buhl remains demonstrates what scientists fear most about NAGPRA's repatriation provisions; that the statute "facilitate[es] destruction of what little evidence does exist that might allow scientists to shed light on who came here when."

Occasionally the archaeologists catch a break and discover exceptional evidence that reveals biological data, and even DNA, about Paleo-Indians without having to test skeletal remains or implicate the repatriation prong of NAGPRA. In the Paisley Caves of Oregon, excavations in 2002 and 2003 revealed fossilized human excrement called coprolites. The coprolites were sent to molecular archaeologists in Copenhagen, Denmark, who were subsequently able to extract viable human mtDNA [mitochondrial DNA; DNA found in part of the cell called mitochondria, rather than in the cell nucleus], and a radiocarbon date from a sample revealed the feces to be nearly 14,300 years old. . . . The ancient leavings from Paisley are the oldest evidence of human habitation in North America and the oldest human DNA obtained from both Americas.

Discoveries like the coprolites at the Paisley Caves are extremely rare, so scientists must necessarily study the physical remains of the Paleo-Indians. . . . However, archaeologists and physical anthropologists recognize that NAGPRA may still be invoked by tribes seeking the repatriation of ancient remains. . . .

Little Salt Spring—Avoiding NAGPRA

In some instances, the mere potential for NAGPRA litigation may even lead to archaeologists intentionally avoiding locations believed to contain human remains. Over 12,000 years ago, Paleo-Indians and Pleistocene animals frequented an hourglass-shaped sinkhole spring in present-day Sarasota County, Florida. As time passed, the water level in the spring rose and buried the previous human occupation sites under silt in an anoxic [low in oxygen] environment that substantially preserved organic material. After 1959, archaeologists began exploring the sinkhole of Little Salt Spring by diving into the water-sheathed time capsule, and several millennia of Florida prehistory came to light.

The divers discovered the shell of an extinct Clovis-era [around 10,000 to 9,000 BC] tortoise with a man-made wooden stake impaling it into the ground. Further, fire-hardened clay recovered from under the shell indicates that the Paleo-Indians likely killed and dined upon the hapless tortoise in the same spot. The archaeologists also recovered several wooden artifacts that dated to the time of the Ancient

One [Native American name for human remains also known as Kennewick Man, found near the Columbia River in Kennewick, Washington]—9,000 years ago—including an oak mortar and a non-returning boomerang likely used for hunting, as well as a spear shaft and a projectile point made from sharpened deer antler. Other artifacts included stone projectile points and wooden tools from the Archaic period, around 6,000 years ago.

The sinkhole further revealed an astonishing find—an ancient graveyard containing an estimated 1,000 human burials. The oldest human remains from Little Salt Springs date to around 6,000 years ago and include well-preserved human brain matter from a skull. Most of the human remains recovered from Little Salt Spring "predate the transfer of ownership to the University of Miami in 1982." Because the university receives federal funding, it would qualify as a "museum" pursuant to NAGPRA, and any human remains raised from the sinkhole would be subject to repatriation. Archaeologists diving at the site have intentionally "avoided excavating any human remains known to exist in various parts of the site" since the fieldwork resumed at Little Salt Spring in 2004.

Though the work at Little Salt Spring escaped the mire of NAGPRA litigation during the past, the archaeologists remain mindful of the act and respectful of the Native American dead. While the divers do not disturb the known Archaic period burials, it is difficult to predict whether they would exhume remains from the Paleoindian level of the site. The researchers have elicited the opinions of Native Americans during several informal consultations regarding the project, which further inculcates the need for cooperation between the two camps. Through additional dialog and compromise, the archaeologists and the Native Americans may devise a plan whereby invaluable information can be gleaned from ancient remains, and then the remains would be repatriated for reburial.

Legal Concerns Hamper Museums' Ability to Comply with NAGPRA

The museum community has serious concerns about the final rule concerning the application of NAGPRA [Native American Graves Protection and Repatriation Act] to culturally unidentifiable human remains and associated funerary objects. As written, the rule would shortchange the consultative process between museums and federally recognized tribes which has made NAGPRA so productive. It exceeds the regulatory authority granted to the Department of the Interior in the original NAGPRA law. It would expose museums to major new legal risks and impose significant new costs above those related to compliance with the original NAGPRA regulations.

Ford W. Bell, American Association of Museums
Letter to Dr. Sherry Hutt, National NAGPRA Program,
May 13, 2010. www.speakupformuseums.org.

Cooperation and Repatriation Without NAGPRA

Conflict between Native Americans and scientists over ancient remains does not always have to be the case. Recall the recent mtDNA study conducted by biologist Ugo Perego and his colleagues. One crucial strand of D4h3a mtDNA [a mitochondrial DNA sequence unique to Native Americans] came from the 10,300-year-old remains of a man discovered in On Your Knees Cave in Alaska's Prince of Wales Island. Upon discovery of the remains, scientists reached out to the local Tlingit and Haida tribes, and the tribes embraced scientific study. Tlingit tribe member and Harvard-trained anthropologist Rosita Worl noted that "[t]he way we interpreted this find was that an ancestor was offering himself to us to give us knowledge." Members of the tribe even assisted in the excavation of the remains from the cave.

Instead of sitting in storage pending the results of litigation for a decade, scientists immediately studied the remains that the locals refer to as Shuka Kaa (Tlingit for "Man Ahead of Us"). Archaeologists learned that Shuka Kaa died in his early twenties and that he lived mostly on a diet of seafood. The seafood results were a bit of a surprise considering the cave in which the remains were discovered is quite some distance from the coast. Based on other artifacts discovered in the cave, scientists theorize that Shuka Kaa's community may have used crude boats to travel between the islands and the mainland, and may even have employed the boats for fishing.

Molecular archaeologists attempted for years to obtain a viable DNA sample from Shuka Kaa's bones with no success. But in 2007, Dr. Brian Kemp of Washington State University tested a tooth and successfully extracted mtDNA. Geneticists analyzed the mtDNA to determine what haplotypes it contained, and were elated to learn that it contained the rare D4h3a strand—the same haplogroup [distinctive genetic pattern] that is only found in populations along the Pacific Coast of South and Central America. Shuka Kaa's DNA proved crucial to Dr. Perego's study and served as solid evidence in support of the coastal route that the first Americans likely followed.

After nearly ten years of providing a wealth of otherwise unobtainable information, Shuka Kaa embarked on one final journey. Dr. Timothy Heaton from the University of South Dakota, who discovered the remains in 1996, escorted the bones back to Alaska for reburial by the Tlingit and Haida tribes. The tribes organized a two-day reburial ceremony, and placed Shuka Kaa to rest in the earth alongside the burials of recent generations of Alaska Natives. Through cooperation, not litigation, archaeologists and Native Americans were able to balance preservation and protection with respect and reverence.

Balancing Protection and Preservation

When the frozen remains of the celebrated Ötzi the Iceman were discovered in the Austrian Alps in 1991, the scientific community was ecstatic. The 5,300-year-old mummified remains and well-preserved artifacts shed invaluable light upon Copper Age Europe at an important time in history where humans were transitioning from stone tools to metallurgy. But for extensive study of the remains, much of the information subsequently gleaned from Ötzi about his time period would have remained unknown or merely theories. It is worth noting that no European community or organization called for the scientists to stop studying the remains or to return the body to them for reburial. Such is not the case in the Americas where the indigenous peoples fight to protect the remains of all of their ancestors, regardless of antiquity.

For Native Americans, the classification of remains as "non-Native American" based merely on a befuddled [US] Ninth Circuit [Court] panel's misreading of the plain language of NAGPRA is both obscene and insulting. However, American anthropologists and archaeologists regard the permanent loss of unique and otherwise unobtainable scientific information as equally obscene and insulting. Where the Native Americans view themselves as the stewards of their faith and their ancestors, the scientists claim to be the stewards of the knowledge of the past. Perhaps the Ninth Circuit thought it was offering a compromise between relatively recent remains and remains of great antiquity. . . .

The Ninth Circuit's compromise was more of a farce because it failed to strike an adequate balance between the competing interests and the holding certainly did not conform to the congressional intent behind NAGPRA. A fair and adequate compromise between preservation and protection is certainly possible, but it will literally take an act of Congress to accomplish effectively. Congress should revisit NAGPRA . . . and amend the act accordingly to specifically address the issue of extremely ancient remains.

First, definition of "Native American" should be broadened to truly encompass the plain meaning of the term, regardless of the antiquity of the remains. Common sense should dictate that any remains found within the United States dating to before 1492 A.D. should be presumed irrefutably to be Native American. Then, Congress should give force and meaning to the aboriginal range repatriation provision of NAGPRA, especially with respect to culturally unidentifiable remains. But in so doing, Congress should also amend the scientific study provision by delineating a definite, set period of time for scientific study of remains to be repatriated, especially if such remains are deemed unaffiliated. In sum, Native American tribes should be afforded a procedure to obtain repatriation of ancient remains subject to necessary scientific study of such remains.

The discovery, study, and eventual reburial of the Prince of Wales Island remains demonstrates how scientists can work together with Native Americans to respectfully study human remains. Archaeologists studying the first Americans should focus on consulting with Native American tribal organizations, especially when they are not required to do so by law, when analyzing ancient remains. With better communication and greater information sharing between the two sides, the study of human remains will seem less like an "us against them" skirmish. Through mutual cooperation, the public will benefit through new and fascinating knowledge about the peopling of the Americas while the tribes will benefit by knowing their ancestors, no matter how remote, will be allowed to rest in peace.

"Glen Cove is the burial ground of our ancestors. It is one of few surviving remnants of our history on this land, so much of which has already been destroyed."

The Glen Cove Development Will Desecrate a Sacred Native American Burial Ground

Sacred Sites Protection and Rights of Indigenous Tribes (SSP&RIT)

Sacred Sites Protection and Rights of Indigenous Tribes (SSP&RIT) is an organization that advocates on behalf of indigenous peoples to protect and preserve sacred sites and the right to engage in traditional Native American spiritual ceremonies, and to cultivate respect for Native American culture and customs. In the following viewpoint, SSP&RIT declares that the proposed development of Glen Cove into a public park violates the human and religious rights of the Native American communities whose ancestors are buried at this site. SSP&RIT provides historical background on the site, detailing not only its spiritual and cultural significance as an ancient Native American burial ground, but also the numerous times that artifacts and human

"About Glen Cove," Sacred Sites Protection and Rights of Indigenous Tribes (SSP&RIT), 2011. Reproduced by permission.

remains have been taken from the area by archaeologists. Glen Cove is a profoundly sacred place to many Native Americans, and the proposed development would not only desecrate the lands by building restrooms and a parking lot on top of burial grounds but also by excavating areas containing graves and sacred objects.

As you read, consider the following questions:

1. When did University of California archeologists first survey Glen Cove, according to the viewpoint?

2. Why do Native Americans object to the use of herbicide and cutting down trees at Glen Cove, according to the viewpoint?

3. In what year does the viewpoint state that the United Nations Declaration on the Rights of Indigenous Peoples was adopted?

Glen Cove is a sacred gathering place and burial ground that has been utilized by numerous Native American tribes since at least 1,500 BC. Today, Glen Cove continues to be spiritually important to local Native communities. It is located just south of Vallejo, California, along the Carquinez Strait, a natural channel that connects the Sacramento River delta to the San Francisco Bay. Glen Cove is known as *Sogorea Te* in Karkin Ohlone language.

Archeologists working for the University of California [UC] first surveyed the Glen Cove site in 1907. Since that time, hundreds of intact skeletal remains and cremations have been documented, along with thousands of sacred objects, tools, and other artifacts. Many sacred items and skeletons unearthed at Glen Cove have been stolen by archeologists and are housed in the Phoebe [A.] Hearst Museum of Anthropology at UC Berkeley.

The 15-acre Glen Cove sacred site is owned by the City of Vallejo and is open to the public as a natural area. A freshwater stream flows through the site and in to tule reeds as it joins with the Carquinez Strait. Much of the inland area is grassland, with native plants such as bulrush and pickleweed concentrated at the waterfront. A large abandoned building known as the Stremmel Mansion (along with an abandoned caretaker's residence) dominates the middle of the site. The Stremmel Mansion is literally built on top of grave sites, and intact shell mounds lie just adjacent to the main building.

A Sacred Burial Ground and Not a Park

Since 1988, the Greater Vallejo Recreation District (GVRD) and the City of Vallejo have been pursuing the development of the Glen Cove site into a "fully featured" public park. GVRD's current master plan calls for the installation of a parking lot, restroom facility, picnic tables, and construction of additional trails, including a paved trail. It also calls for re-grading of large areas of the site, which involves digging that will further disturb burials and sacred objects. This planned grading includes "capping" known shell mound–burial areas with 12 inches of soil.

The local Native American community has been outspoken for over ten years about the Glen Cove sacred site, and the message has been overwhelmingly: *Do not further disturb and manipulate this sacred burial ground of our ancestors.* It is not a park. Spiritual leaders from Ohlone, Miwok, Pomo and other local tribes consider the proposed park development plans to be an offensive desecration of this holy area that has already seen many years of abuse in the hands of settlers. Furthermore, we consider the manipulation of our ancestors' burial site without our informed consent to be *a violation of our human and religious rights.*

The master plan also calls for an aggressive extermination of non-native plant species. Procedures detailed in the plan describe cutting down trees and applying herbicide to their exposed trunks and remaining root systems. The plan also calls for years of ongoing herbicide application. Elders in the local Native community say that *All Life is Sacred*. We oppose extermination of the trees and plants that have taken root on this sacred burial ground, regardless of whether they are endemic species or relative newcomers.

The Right to Maintain and Protect

The Greater Vallejo Recreation District and City of Vallejo claim that their plans for park development take the Native community into consideration. On paper, it is diplomatically acknowledged that "sensitive cultural resources" exist at Glen Cove. However, no real effort has been made to involve the local Native community in decision making. Despite years of phone calls, letters, and even demonstrations ending at GVRD headquarters to deliver stacks of petitions, the agency maintains that the wishes of Native Americans regarding Glen Cove are "unclear."

Steve Pressley, a manager for GVRD, states in regard to Glen Cove that "*as an agency, we have a responsibility to the public as a whole, and we need to consider all the components, not just the needs of Native Americans.*" This attitude sidesteps two basic truths. Firstly, the entire Bay Area including Vallejo was illegitimately stolen from the Native people, who now have no land base because our very existence in the present day continues to be denied by the federal government in most cases. Secondly, the relationship of local Native people with Glen Cove is fundamentally distinct from that of other members of the public, for Glen Cove is the burial ground of our ancestors. It is one of few surviving remnants of our history on this land, so much of which has already been destroyed or paved over without regard for our people.

Therefore, rather than being one group among many who is considered in deciding the fate of Glen Cove, we assert that

The Proposed Development of Glen Cove Would Violate the Law

The desecration of burial mounds such as Glen Cove and the theft of human remains is a criminal act that seems to be tolerated when it comes to indigenous remains. Yet this is in blatant disregard of the Native American Graves Protection and Repatriation Act (NAGPRA) of 1990, which mandates indigenous human remains are to be afforded the same protection as other human remains, in recognition of the federal treaties that acknowledge sovereignty.

Sean Jobst, "Desecration of Glen Cove Burial Mounds
Reveals Blatant Disregard for Humanity," Initium,
or How I Learned to Love the Kali-Yuga,
May 9, 2011. http://kali-yuga.org.

the local Native community should rightfully be the lead decision maker who holds authority in matters related to our sacred burial ground.

The UN Declaration on the Rights of Indigenous Peoples

Guidance may be offered by the United Nations [UN] Declaration on the Rights of Indigenous Peoples, adopted in 2007, which states:

- Indigenous peoples have the right to manifest, practice, develop and teach their spiritual and religious traditions, customs and ceremonies; *the right to maintain, protect, and have access in privacy to their religious and cultural sites*; the right to the use and control of their ceremonial objects; and the right to the repatriation of their human remains. (Article 12)

- Indigenous peoples have the right to maintain and strengthen their distinctive spiritual relationship with their traditionally owned or otherwise occupied and used lands, territories, waters and coastal seas and other resources and to uphold their responsibilities to future generations in this regard. (Article 25)

- Indigenous peoples have the right to practice and revitalize their cultural traditions and customs. This includes the right to maintain, protect and develop the past, present and future manifestations of their cultures, such as archaeological and historical sites, artifacts, designs, ceremonies, technologies and visual and performing arts and literature. (Article 11, part 1)

- States shall provide redress through effective mechanisms, which may include restitution, developed in conjunction with indigenous peoples, with respect to their cultural, intellectual, religious and spiritual property taken without their free, prior and informed consent or in violation of their laws, traditions and customs. (Article 11, part 2)

Stopping Any Further Development Is of the Utmost Importance

We are asking you to stop and think about how important this area is to our youth and community as a whole. Can you imagine the historical significance of this sacred site, and what this means? Even if you somehow cannot identify with the disregard for the dignity of the ancient people and items buried there, you must see the significance of the historical value of this place. It is one of the last remaining shell mounds in the north Bay Area, and older than the pyramids of Egypt.

Please give us your support. Get your signature on our petitions, come to our gatherings and meet the descendants of this sacred place. And most importantly, get the word out.

Talk to your neighbors, coworkers and friends about respecting sacred sites and the rights of indigenous people.

> "[The Greater Vallejo Recreation
> District's] plan is designed to protect
> and preserve the site, not desecrate it."

The Glen Cove Development Will Not Disrupt or Desecrate a Sacred Native American Burial Ground

Janet Roberson

Janet Roberson is the former vice chairperson of the Greater Vallejo Recreation District (GVRD) board of directors and a resident of Vallejo, California. In the following viewpoint, Roberson refutes Native American community claims that the proposed development of the Glen Cove site involves creating a public park and destroying a sacred Native American burial ground. The development plan, according to Roberson, is to restore the land and preserve its natural state, and not to dig up or pave the grounds to create a lavish public park. Roberson insists that the developers have taken pains to research the site to avoid disturbing culturally sensitive areas within the site, and that the planned improvements, such as regrading and repairing the drainage and sewer systems, removing trip hazards, and making hidden areas

Janet Roberson, "Glen Cove Site: Separating Fact from Fiction," *Vallejo Times-Herald*, April 21, 2011. Reproduced by permission.

visible to surrounding neighbors to discourage dangerous or criminal activity, are essential to maintain the integrity of the site and ensure that it is safe. Roberson maintains that the new construction of additional parking lots and restrooms will be completed in an area of the site that has not been designated as culturally sensitive, and the GVRD has an obligation to provide adequate parking and bathroom facilities to those who visit the area. Roberson also argues that the plan for Glen Cove has been heartily endorsed by several individuals in the Native American community and that a Native American anthropology expert has hailed the plan as a model for preserving other such sites.

As you read, consider the following questions:

1. What are the problems created by overgrown plants in the Glen Cove site, according to Roberson?

2. What does the graffiti at Glen Cove declare, according to Roberson?

3. What does the viewpoint state is the tribal affiliation of the "Most Likely Descendant"?

There have been many recent news reports regarding the waterfront land at Glen Cove, which contains a natural, historic treasure of 15 unspoiled acres along the Carquinez [Strait] shoreline. This land is owned by the City of Vallejo and managed by the Greater Vallejo Recreation District [GVRD]. It appears that many people have been misled by activists who are spreading misinformation. It might interest your readers to know the following information—the facts and the fiction—which has been compiled by many of us who live next to the land and have taken great interest in this issue.

GVRD plans to develop this land as a park—Fiction.

For years this land was planned to be developed as an elaborate park, with concession stands, swimming piers, and manicured lawns. Our community worked together with

GVRD to make sure this land would not be developed, but rather preserved and restored to its natural condition.

The land cannot be left as it is—Fact.

Sadly, for many years this land has been neglected, allowing invasive plants to choke out native species, causing a jungle-like atmosphere that has encouraged a variety of nefarious activities and significant fire hazard during the dry season. Additionally, safety issues have to be addressed, such as improper grading and drainage issues, standing water (with mosquito infestation), sewer system remnants (human waste seepage), protruding rebar, "trip-and-fall" hazards, abandoned structures, and other safety and liability concerns. Furthermore, the regrading will allow homeowners to see areas of the site that are currently hidden where nefarious activity currently takes place. This will make the entire area safer and eliminate liability issues for which the city would be responsible.

Preservation and Not Desecration

The land will be desecrated and bodies will be dug up—Fiction.

This is simply untrue. GVRD's plan is designed to protect and preserve the site, not desecrate it. Extra steps have been taken to protect the culturally sensitive area, including covering it with additional soil. There will be no digging in this portion of the site. Significant time and expense have gone into careful research, including core sampling and consultation with experts in the field to ensure there will be no disturbance of any archaeologically significant areas. This beautiful area has been desecrated, however, by vandals who have defaced the site with extensive graffiti declaring "sacred burial ground" (often misspelled) and other similar phrases.

The city is bankrupt and can't afford it—Fiction.

The funding for the necessary safety improvements for this site has been provided by grant money that is not related to the City of Vallejo. The notion that the city is broke and this grant money can be spent elsewhere is not an option. It cannot be allocated elsewhere. If it is not spent on the preservation of this site, it will be forfeited.

Bathrooms and parking lots are being built over a sacred burial ground—Fiction.

The additional parking and restrooms that are planned have purposely been kept as small and unobtrusive as possible, and are not located on the area of the site that has been identified as culturally sensitive. GVRD has an obligation to all citizens of Vallejo and cannot ignore that people who wish to visit this site to pay their respects need a place to park and a place to relieve themselves.

This obligation has been proven over the past several days as dozens of cars have been illegally parked near the entrance to the site, due to the lack of ample parking spaces. Furthermore, activists who have set up camp in the area have erected unpermitted portable restrooms in close proximity to where the small permanent restroom is planned, showing that even those who claim they are offended by the planned restrooms need them and have put porta-potties over land they have labeled as sacred.

Funding Is Sufficient and Support Is Widespread

There will be no money to maintain the new bathrooms—Fiction.

GVRD maintains 35 separate recreational facilities, nature areas, and parks, many of which have bathroom facilities. The additional maintenance of one bathroom facility can readily be supported within existing operational resources with minimal additional effort, considering there is one such facility that is currently being maintained a short distance from this site. GVRD will add this site to the daily park maintenance route at minimal expense to the district. It should be noted that GVRD has worked within its budget over the past few

The Glen Cove Development Respects and Safeguards Native America Resources and Culture

The [Glen Cove] project will not damage or desecrate Native American remains or resources on the site....

No development will occur in the documented cultural resources area.... No digging or ground disturbance will occur in the cultural resources protection area.... Only non-native trees are being removed, and this will be done by cutting off above ground, without disturbing the roots or soil.

Shane McAffee and Phil Batchelor,
Letter to Norman "Wounded Knee" DeOcampo,
April 18, 2011. www.glencovenaturearea.org.

years, despite significant funding decreases, continuing to maintain and refurbish the restrooms and facilities in existing parks. Their track record of allocating their resources wisely is praiseworthy and remarkable, especially in these difficult economic times.

GVRD's plan is supported by Native Americans—Fact.

The Native American representative designated by the California Native American Heritage [Commission] supports GVRD's plan. The Most Likely Descendant (based on archaeological records), who is of the Rumsey Band of Wintun Indians, supports the current plans for this land and resents those who have interfered with the progress of GVRD's plan. The tribe has approved and is supportive of the project. Their designated cultural resources coordinator has been actively involved in monitoring the site testing, and will be present for future work.

Experts recommend that GVRD's plan be a model for the protection of other culturally sensitive sites—Fact.

GVRD's plan has been hailed by an expert on North American anthropology as "a model for site protection that should be applied across the greater San Francisco Bay Area." This expert, a professor of anthropology at the University of California, Berkeley, and interim director of the Phoebe [A.] Hearst Museum of Anthropology, was selected by the Vallejo Inter-Tribal Council as an expert to examine GVRD's plan. All of his suggestions were followed and placed into the preservation plan.

Periodical and Internet Sources Bibliography

The following articles have been selected to supplement the diverse views presented in this chapter.

Gavin Aronsen	"Will Big Solar Bulldoze Sacred Tribal Sites?," *Mother Jones*, April 1, 2011.
Glynn Custred	"Origin Story," *National Review Online*, March 19, 2009. www.nationalreview.com.
David Danelski	"California Desert: Native Americans Object to Energy Projects," *Press-Enterprise*, October 19, 2010.
Søren Holm	"Removing Bodies from Display Is Nonsense," *New Scientist*, March 16, 2011.
Van Jones, Bracken Hendricks, and Jorge Madrid	"Clearing the Way for a Native Opportunity in America's 'Sputnik Moment,'" Center for American Progress, January 27, 2011. www.americanprogress.org.
David Kimelberg	"A Chance to Right a Wrong: The Seneca Nation of Indians and the Kinzua Dam," Indian Country Today Media Network, January 28, 2011. http://indiancountrytodaymedia network.com.
Monique La Chappa	"Pro: Clean, Renewable Wind Energy Benefits All," *San Diego Union Tribune*, February 13, 2011.
Keith Matheny	"Solar Energy Plans Pit Green vs. Green," *USA Today*, June 2, 2011.

CHAPTER 4

What Economic Factors Most Concern Native Americans?

Chapter Preface

The portion of Native American communities living in poverty on reservations has been consistently as high as 25 percent,[1] with unemployment on the Blackfoot reservation in Montana at times exceeding 69 percent.[2] Experts explain that decade after decade of extreme poverty, combined with physical isolation and the destruction of Native American culture, has resulted in widespread depression, alcoholism, drug addiction, and a suicide rate that in a 2004 report by the US Commission on Civil Rights is posted as 190 percent of the national average and rising.[3] The report also relates that the highest rate of suicide among Native Americans is among young people—it is the second leading cause of death for those aged fifteen to twenty-four and the third leading cause of death for those aged five to fourteen. These rates, the report continues, are "twice as great among 14- to 24-year-olds, and three times as great among 5- to 10-year-olds, as it was in the general population."

"The young go to movies, watch television and they see all of the modern technology that comes with cell phones, iPods, and iPads. They are exposed to the world of texting and tweeting, but find they are unable to afford these innovative technologies because of extreme poverty and oftentimes from the distance and isolation of their Indian reservations. This deprivation can instill depression in the young," asserts Tim Giago in a *Huffington Post* article discussing the high suicide rate on reservations.[4] Giago reports that the generations of Native Americans born on reservations who were sent away from their homes to live in boarding schools that sought to systematically destroy their ties to their native culture and indoctrinate them into Christianity and white society have grown up increasingly alienated from, and even ashamed of, their heritage and spiritual traditions. This devastation of their culture,

Giago explains, has led to substance abuse and family violence, which, when they are combined "with extreme poverty . . . [sow] the seeds of extreme depression." Tribal elders and aid organizations have had some success by addressing the suicide epidemic, Giago notes, with outreach efforts that increase young Native Americans' involvement and pride in their culture and spiritual traditions, but these efforts are limited and often thwarted by a lack of funding for such necessities as facilities and the costs involved in training employees. The links between culture, tradition, and economics is explained by Doug Cuthand in a column addressing the suicide rate for "First Nations youth" in Canada that is "five to seven times higher than the national average." Cuthand declares, "Research has shown that communities where the culture is strong have a lower rate of suicide compared to reserves where the culture has been lost or seriously weakened. Also, when employment rates increase, the suicide rate declines."[5]

According to the 2004 US Civil Rights Commission report, Native American communities face a far greater need for mental health services than the general population, but this need is exacerbated by far less access to services than what is available to the general population. Senator Byron Dorgan of North Dakota, who chairs the Senate Committee on Indian Affairs, began an investigation into the Indian Health Service after a rash of suicides took place on the Standing Rock reservation located in both North and South Dakota in 2009. Among other things, Dorgan's investigation revealed that a vacancy for the director of mental health on the reservation went unfilled for more than a year. Dorgan declared, "That represents, in my judgment, incompetence. The Indian Health Service has a responsibility to fill these positions and make mental health treatment available to people." He added, "I think Congress has some responsibility to provide more funding here."[6] Dorgan later sponsored a bill to fund improvements in the Indian Health Service in general and in mental health services in particular that eventually became part of the Patient Protection and Affordable Care Act that was signed into law by President Barack Obama in 2010.

The extraordinarily high suicide rate among Native Americans is one of many consequences of economic hardships faced by this group. In the following chapter, authors of the viewpoints explore economic issues of greatest concern to Native Americans, including the settlement of the historic federal lawsuit *Cobell v. Salazar*; the effects of Native American casinos on state and local economies; and the debate over whether government assistance helps or worsens Native American poverty.

Notes

1. "American Indian and Alaska Native Heritage," US Census Bureau, September 1, 2009. www.census.gov.
2. Tom Rodgers, "Native American Poverty," *Spotlight on Poverty and Opportunity*, December 10, 2008. www.spotlight onpoverty.org.
3. US Commission on Civil Rights, "Broken Promises: Evaluating the Native American Health Care System," September 2004.
4. Tim Giago, "High Suicide Rate on Indian Reservation Near Epidemic Proportions," *Huffington Post*, June 1, 2010. www .huffingtonpost.com.
5. Doug Cuthand, weekly column from *Saskatchewan Leader-Post*, February 9, 2009, reproduced in "Youth Suicide Among Native Americans Linked to Colonialism," *Suicide Prevention News and Comment*, February 9, 2009. http://suicide preventioncommunity.wordpress.com.
6. Allie Tempus, "A Tribal Tragedy: High Native American Suicide Rates Persist," WisconsinWatch.org, November 21, 2010. www.wisconsinwatch.org.

> *"It is now important that we implement this historical settlement. . . . Hundreds of thousands of individual Indians have waited patiently for far too long."*

The *Cobell v. Salazar* Settlement Provides Critical Funds to Native Americans

Elouise P. Cobell

Elouise P. Cobell is a banker and rancher, a member of the Blackfeet Indian tribe of Montana, and the lead plaintiff in the case that eventually became known as Cobell v. Salazar, *which challenged the US government's mismanagement of Indian trust funds. Cobell served as treasurer of the Blackfeet tribe, and she established the Blackfeet National Bank, the first national bank located on an Indian reservation and owned by a Native American tribe. In the following viewpoint, Cobell remarks upon the settlement of the* Cobell v. Salazar *case, asserting that while the $3.4 billion settlement falls short of the total amount the US government owes to the Native American people, it was necessary to reach a compromise in order to provide assistance to in-*

Elouise P. Cobell, "Statement of Elouise P. Cobell, Lead Plaintiff in *Cobell v. Salazar*," Proposed Settlement of the *Cobell v. Salazar* Litigation Oversight Hearing Before the Committee on Natural Resources, US House of Representatives, Committee on Natural Resources, United States House of Representatives, March 10, 2010, pp. 53–56.

dividual Native Americans, many of whom are living in abject poverty. Additionally, Cobell notes, several key initiatives will be funded with the settlement, which will also help to usher in desperately needed reforms in the government's handling of the Indian trust fund. Cobell asserts that common criticisms of the settlement are based on misinformation and affirms that both the terms of the settlement and the disbursement of settlement funds are equitable and competently managed.

As you read, consider the following questions:

1. What was the initial name of the case that ultimately became *Cobell v. Salazar*, according to the viewpoint?

2. What is the least amount of money that each individual beneficiary of the settlement will receive, according to Cobell?

3. According to the viewpoint, what percentage of the total settlement did the attorneys for the plaintiffs agree to accept as payment?

I am here today [March 10, 2010] representing a class of over 500,000 individual Indians as the lead plaintiff in the case initially entitled *Cobell v. Babbitt* and now referred to as *Cobell v. Salazar*, pending in the United States District Court for the District of Columbia and presently presided over by Judge James Robertson. Since virtually its inception more than 13 years ago, Congress has taken keen interest in this litigation and its key objectives—reforming the individual Indian trust, ensuring that the government accounts for all trust assets including all trust funds, land and natural resources, and correcting and restating each individual's account balance.

By any measure, this litigation has proven exceptional and extraordinary. Not only is it one of the largest class actions ever brought against the United States as it addresses over 120 years of mismanagement of Indian trust assets and involves over 500,000 individual Indians, but the litigation has been intense and contentious. Moreover, there have been more than 3600 docket entries in the district court and over 80 published decisions, including ten appeals—the most recent appellate opinion is referred to as Cobell XXII.

Compromising to Provide Essential Resources and Reforms

On each occasion I have appeared before Congress, I have emphasized my willingness to explore settlement of this case. But of course, resolution takes two parties willing to come to the table to negotiate in good faith and attempt to reach an equitable settlement that would set the foundation for improved trust management and accountability in the future. Until very recently, however, we did not have such a willing partner on the other side. President [Barack] Obama showed great leadership during the campaign when he committed to seek a fair resolution to this case and, when elected, he followed through and charged [Interior] Secretary [Ken] Salazar and Attorney General [Eric] Holder with carrying out this commitment.

Having been through seven failed settlement efforts before, I was not optimistic at the outset of these negotiations that we would be able to reach agreement. Beginning in the late summer of 2009, though, we sat down in good faith and so did the administration. Associate Attorney General Tom Perrelli, Interior Deputy Secretary David Hayes, and Interior Solicitor Hilary Tompkins were involved in the day-to-day negotiations. The issues to discuss and resolve were gravely challenging, and I repeatedly felt we had reached impasse. But both my team and the government soldiered on, knowing that resolution was the best thing for the affected individual Indian trust beneficiaries and for a healthier foundation of the trust relationship for the future.

Reaching agreement was certainly not easy, and the settlement from my perspective is not perfect. I would want more for beneficiaries as I think that is what they deserve. But a settlement requires compromise—by definition, you do not get everything you want. This is the bottom line: After months of discussion, I am here to testify that I strongly support this agreement. It is time to look forward, not backward. And though we must never forget the past, this settlement can move us forward together as it represents the best resolution we can hope for under the circumstances.

Although we have reached an historical settlement totaling more than $3.4 billion, there is little doubt this is far less than the full amount to which individual Indians are entitled. Yes, we could prolong our struggle, fight longer, and, perhaps one day, reach a judgment in the courts that results in a greater benefit to individual Indians. But we are nevertheless compelled to settle now by the sobering reality that members of our class die each year, each month, and every day, forever prevented from receiving that which is theirs. We also face the uncomfortable, but unavoidable fact that a large number of individual Indian trust beneficiaries are among the most vulnerable people in this country, existing in the direst of poverty. This settlement can begin to provide hope and a much-needed measure of justice.

In addition, now that the *Cobell* case has brought heightened attention to this matter, I am optimistic that this settlement will lay the foundation for genuine and meaningful reform of the trust. There remains considerable room for improvement, as Secretary Salazar and Deputy Secretary Hayes have recognized. I am hopeful that the commission that Secretary Salazar has contemporaneously announced with this settlement will ensure that additional critical reforms are made and that we set the underpinning for safe and sound management of our assets in the future.

Individual Native Americans Will Receive Substantial Funds

The terms of the settlement have been well publicized. We have reached out to Indian country to insure that beneficiaries are well informed of its terms. I just returned from meeting with beneficiaries in South Dakota, and our class counsel, as we speak, is traveling to meet with beneficiaries in other states. We have met with allottee associations, tribal organizations and landowners and will continue our efforts. Next week, our class counsel will visit Arizona and New Mexico, the following week Montana, Wyoming and North Dakota and the weeks after that Oklahoma, Washington, California and Oregon. Further meetings with beneficiaries will continue throughout Indian country in March and April to make sure that they are able to receive complete and accurate information about the settlement.

Despite this outreach, there remains misinformation regarding the settlement conveyed by a very small number of individuals, many of whom are not beneficiaries and do not speak for individual Indian beneficiaries. I want to dispel those misunderstandings.

First, there are those who have stated that under this agreement beneficiaries will receive very little. This is not accurate. In fact, most beneficiaries who participate in this settlement will receive at least—and I emphasize at least—$1,500.00. Many will receive substantially more based on the transactional activity in their IIM [individual Indian money] account. To those in Indian country, receipt of this money is critical, both as a recognition of the government's past wrongdoing and as a first step in fulfilling the commitment to reforming the trust system. Many individual Indians are dependent on this money for the basic necessities of life. Its payment should not be further delayed.

Two other points are important with respect to these distributions. First, receipt of these funds shall not be construed as income and thus will not be taxable for beneficiaries. This is only fair because proceeds from trust lands are generally not taxable. Second, and critically important to the poorest among the class, the *Cobell* settlement funds shall not be considered when determining eligibility for programs such as TANF [Temporary Assistance for Needy Families], SSI [Supplemental Security Income] and food stamps. The last thing the parties want is to further victimize poorer class members by preventing them from receiving benefits from programs for which they would otherwise be eligible.

Second, there are suggestions that the settlement should not have encompassed claims for trust administration since it is contended the *Cobell* case did not involve mismanagement of trust assets. This is not correct. The *Cobell* case has always insisted that the government account for all trust assets—not just money but the land and natural resources that are at the heart of the individual Indian trust. And, the district court invited plaintiffs to amend our complaint to include these claims in the litigation well before these settlement negotiations. In other words, their inclusion should be no surprise. Indeed, while true that there are certain trust damages claims that are now expressly included that were not before, understand that virtually all settlement discussions—including those led by this committee [referring to the US House Committee on Natural Resources] and the Senate Indian Affairs Committee—have contemplated the inclusion of all such individual claims. The largest and oldest tribal organization, the National Congress of American Indians, passed unanimously a resolution in 2006 endorsing inclusion of all trust management claims if, whereas here, there is an opt out.

I and others were also counseled on this point by the following sober reality: Very few trust mismanagement cases have ever been filed and those that have are very expensive, extremely time consuming and fraught with risk. There is an obvious reason for this. For most beneficiaries, the claims are relatively modest when compared with the cost of litigating against the government and the legal obstacles in doing so. Legal hindrances abound, such as statute of limitations and jurisdictional restrictions, and together with the cost prohibitive nature of litigation, help explain why so few have been brought. For the great majority of beneficiaries, this settlement represents the only opportunity for them to receive any compensation for the government's mismanagement of their trust assets. For those who wish to pursue those claims independently, they have the opportunity to do so by opting out of the trust administration portion of the settlement. The agreement preserves all legal mechanisms to enable them to do so.

All Plaintiffs and Attorneys Are Entitled to Their Share

Third, there are those who criticize the amount that the class attorneys may receive by reason of this settlement. That criticism is misplaced. This is not a case where attorneys are attempting to get a fee based on a quick settlement. The attorneys in this case undertook substantial risk in filing and prosecuting this case on behalf of the 500,000 individual Indian beneficiaries in 1996. Many of the attorneys gave up their practices to work solely on it. It has often consumed 18-hour days, seven days a week. They have engaged in seven major trials, handled countless appeals by the government and reviewed tens of millions of pages of documents. They responded when no on else—not even Congress—was able to correct the wrongdoing that individual Indians endured. As a result of their efforts, for the first time in over 100 years, the government has been held accountable for its mismanagement of the IIM trust. Moreover, solely as a result of their efforts, reform of the trust is a real possibility. The benefit to class members from their efforts is considerable. They have agreed to limit their petition for fees to under $100 million. This is less than 3% of the total settlement—very modest when compared with fees typically awarded in class actions. Class members will have the opportunity to object to the fees and those objections will be considered by the court before any fee award. The attempt by some such as ITMA [Intertribal Monitoring Association] to limit the fees further to those available under the Equal Access to Justice Act (EAJA) suffers from two infirmities. First, the government has made clear that it is not open to paying fees through EAJA. Second, if in the end, lawyer fees are so dramatically curtailed, then how will individual Indians ever obtain the kind of highly competent and dedicated counsel necessary to bring a difficult case like this next time? It is already tragically difficult to attract such lawyers and ITMA would like to make it all the more challenging. This makes no sense.

Fourth, there are those that have even suggested that the named plaintiffs in this case, including me, will profit from this settlement. This again is erroneous. The incentive fee contemplated is an award to named plaintiffs by the court for their work in assisting in this case and to cover expenses. As you might expect, the work required has been considerable. However, most of the money requested will be for reimbursement of expenses incurred during the 14 years of this litigation. Millions of dollars have been spent in prosecuting this case, including payment of experts, and covering charges for transcripts and other court costs. I have contributed substantial funds to aid in the prosecution of this case. The Blackfeet Reservation Development Fund, a nonprofit, has used millions of its own funds as well. Furthermore, many of the grants we received are in the form of loans and are repayable. Importantly, any class members not comfortable with the incentive award will have an opportunity to have their views heard by the court before any payment is made. However, those who have advanced the money to prosecute this case deserve to be reimbursed.

Finally, some who don't understand the reality of the historical data and the lack of reliable information, have criticized the distribution scheme contemplated in this settlement. They say it doesn't track with precision the losses for each beneficiary. The reality is that there is no data to establish actual losses. This is indeed rough justice. But it is the best possible way to achieve three important objectives: (1) being fair so that all receive a meaningful payment of at least $1,500, while rewarding high dollar accounts that likely suffered the most losses; (2) permitting for a prompt distribution where most beneficiaries will be completely paid within a few months; and (3) will not waste significant money on lawyers, accountants and special masters trying to figure out what is owed to each individual. In addition, the court will hear any objections to the distribution scheme and make a determination on its fairness.

Some have asked to establish an extensive and expensive process where beneficiaries can have essentially mini-trials before a special master. This is absolutely and unequivocally foolish. It would waste significant funds on figuring out who gets what and will take years before beneficiaries receive their distributions. Moreover, it will not be advantageous to those beneficiaries who can prove their case since such beneficiaries have the ability to opt out anyway and pursue their claims independently. In short, such a proposal would take years, cost hundreds of millions and be no fairer than the current model. This is precisely why the parties rejected such an approach.

The Settlement Is an Important Milestone but Not a Cure-All

In summary, this settlement will do a lot of good. It will get more than $3 billion in the hands of beneficiaries. It will provide monies for land consolidation. It will create a $60 million scholarship fund. Moreover, there will be a secretarial commission to recommend additional trust reforms that are desperately needed. And there is an agreement to perform an audit of the trust. No audit has ever been done. To heal the division between individual Indian trust beneficiaries and the government that is reflected historically and in the nearly 14 years of our litigation and to begin to establish confidence that the IIM trust is managed in accordance with trust law, transparency is essential. Too many records have been destroyed. Too much deception has occurred. Importantly, this settlement will allow individual Indians to look forward and work collaboratively with their trustee to ensure a better tomorrow.

We know this settlement does not solve many of the serious underlying problems plaguing this trust. We know that reform must continue and cannot stop here. We will continue our efforts to ensure accountability. We have had to spend too much time looking backwards, trying to address the terrible wrongs of the past. Now, my hope is that we look forward to correct those wrongs so that individual Indian trust beneficiaries finally receive that which rightfully is theirs.

When I embarked on this settlement process, I was skeptical that this result could be achieved. But we were able to reach a resolution. There has been too much discussion about what we would like to achieve for individual Indian beneficiaries. It is now important that we implement this historical settlement. I now ask Congress to swiftly enact the necessary implementing legislation so we can begin to distribute our trust funds without further delay. Hundreds of thousands of individual Indians have waited patiently for far too long.

> "It is utterly inappropriate for the historic perpetrators of harms to name their own laws ... and to exclude any role for the sovereign laws and judicial and executive powers of those who suffered the harms."

The *Cobell v. Salazar* Settlement Offers Inadequate Compensation and Lacks Important Provisions

Edward Charles Valandra

Edward Charles Valandra is Sicangu Titunwan and is the founder of the Community for the Advancement of Native Studies, an independent Native research organization. He is the author of the book Not Without Our Consent: Lakota Resistance to Termination, 1950–59. *In the following viewpoint, Valandra advances numerous objections to the* Cobell v. Salazar *settlement, asserting that it violates the human rights of citizens of the Native American Oceti Sakowin Oyate nation (People of the Seven Council Fires who speak Dakota, Lakota, and Nakota, the three dialects of this nation, also known as the "Great Sioux*

Edward Charles Valandra, "Objections to the Settlement *Cobell v. Salazar,* Prepared by Community for the Advancement of Native Studies," *Lakota Country Times,* February 2011. Reproduced by permission of the author.

*Nation") and offers compensation that is not only wholly insuf-
ficient to meet the needs of struggling Native American communities but also represents only a tiny fraction of what they are
owed. Furthermore, Valandra declares, too much settlement
money is diverted to non–Native Americans and offers no provisions for making amends for past wrongs that have been committed against Native Americans or for legally protecting them
from future exploitation. The settlement, according to Valandra,
disrespects Native Americans, ignores history, and threatens to
further disenfranchise Native people, robbing them of their rights,
land, and resources.*

As you read, consider the following questions:

1. According to the author, what did US attorney general
   Alberto Gonzalez testify was the dollar amount of the
   mismanaged Indian trust fund assets?

2. Why, according to Valandra, should the widespread killing of buffalo by non–Native Americans be characterized as an act of genocide?

3. What did the 1962 lawsuit *Running Horse et al. v. Udall*
   show, according to the author?

Preamble: On 8 December 2010 the Americans' leader, President [Barack] Obama, and the plaintiffs in the *Cobell v.
Salazar* lawsuit agreed to an out-of-court settlement. According to a court authorized notice, class members can object to
the settlement:

A class member who wishes to object to the fairness, rea-
sonableness or adequacy of this agreement or of the settlement contemplated hereby must file with the Clerk of the
Court and serve on the Parties a statement of the objection
setting forth the specific reason(s), if any, for the objection,
including any legal support that the class member wishes to
bring to the court's attention, any evidence that the class
member wishes to introduce in support of the objection, any
grounds to support his or her status as a class member.

As a member of the Historical Accounting Class, I am filing my objections in regards to the following terms of agreement:

Settlement Background Nos. 1, 2, 4, 5, 8, 9, 10, 15, 16, and 17;

Terms of Agreement:

A. Definitions Nos. 1, 15, 16, 19, and 20;

B. Amended Complaint and Preliminary Approval No. 1;

C. Class Notice and Opt Out No. 2;

D. Motion for Judgment, Fairness Hearing, and Final Approval Nos. 2 and 3;

E. Accounting/Trust Administration Fund No. 3;

F. Trust Land Consolidation Fund Nos. 1, 2, 3, and 4;

I. Releases 1, 2, and 8;

J. Attorney Fees;

K. Class Representatives' Incentive Awards No. 8;

L. No Further Monetary Obligation 1, 2, 3(2), and 9.

These objections to the settlement are not exhaustive, however. They are representative of the unresolved historic claims of the Oceti Sakowin Oyate citizens (herein Oyate) against the American people, through their government. These claims remain outstanding with respect to the mismanagement of our trust assets and the breach of Americans' trust responsibilities to Native peoples. I now come forward to state the reasons for my objections to the settlement.

Depriving Us of Our Rights and Failing to Meet Their Obligations

1. There is no provision in the settlement that permits opting out of agreement. The agreement prohibits the Historical Accounting Class, unlike the Trust Administration Class, from

opting out. This prohibition violates human rights standards, because it denies individuals the opportunity to voluntarily exclude themselves from the agreement. This prohibition also violates consent clauses that the Oyate demanded in its treaties with the Americans, to which they agreed. These consent clauses are foundational; they recognize that individuals of the Oyate are guaranteed a voice in matters that impact them, their families, and their nation. The settlement provides that, as a Historical Accounting Class member, I am involuntarily relinquishing my right to sue the US for claims being resolved by the settlement. Of course, this relinquishment means that my descendants are also barred from suing the American people as well. More egregious is that the Americans, through their government, deny all these claims despite the evidence to the contrary! The settlement says that the American people have *no* legal responsibilities for these claims and *owes* nothing to the class members. This American position is comparable to Germans saying that they have no legal responsibilities and owe nothing to Jewish people who suffered during the Holocaust.

2. The $3.4 billion settlement is grossly inadequate to restore the lives of Native allottees. The settlement amount is inadequate to repair the social, political, health, and economic harms caused by American colonization viz the Bureau of Indian Affairs and other American institutions. In March 2005, US Attorney General [Alberto] Gonzales testified to a House Committee that Americans faced a $200 billion liability because their government has mismanaged colonized trust assets—the IIM [individual Indian money] accounts of Native peoples—since 1887. That the settlement was reduced to $3.4 billion—not even two percent of the amount legally and rightfully due Native landholders—is outrageous. The theft of $196.6 billion from Native people is all the more egregious considering that in October 2008 Congress authorized $700 billion under the Emergency Economic Stabilization Act to

bail out the very people and organizations that caused economic hardship in the US. In short, Americans in power reward individuals and organizations that are criminally irresponsible toward the less powerful.

Non–Native Americans Profit from Our Settlement

3. The class-action suit counsel is awarded money from settlement funds. According to the settlement, the attorneys' fees, costs and expenses, which range from a minimum of $99.9 million to a maximum of $223 million, must be paid from the awarded settlement amount. Here again, Native peoples are victimized by the colonizers' justice system. The American officials who perpetuated the massive fraud and mismanagement of Native trust assets must pay the class counsel, not the allottees or their heirs. In similar liability suits, counsel seeks remuneration not from their clients but from the individuals or organizations that harmed their client(s). It would be disingenuous for a court to award a victim and then give a significant percentage of the award to the victim's counsel. Traditionally, the offender—the person(s) or organization(s) who committed the harm—is required to remunerate the victim's counsel.

4. There is no provision in the settlement protecting the Oyate's future claims. The settlement fails to protect any future claims made by the Oyate against the US regarding treaty lands that were subject to the allotment act. This settlement does not contain language that protects or hold harmless any treaty land from the releases. Since treaty lands are held in trust or restricted status, any future claims by the Historical Accounting Class against historic wrongs and past harms by the US are prohibited. Since the allotment act privatized our national lands, the settlement has circumscribed the Oyate's collective interest in what was originally treaty land. Accepting the settlement means individuals—and this would include

their descendants—can no longer file any further suits regarding breach of trust. Meanwhile the settlement permits the Americans to avoid any admission of guilt or wrongdoing.

5. There is no provision in the settlement for land reform and restoration program. The $1.9 billion allocated to purchase fractionated Indian trust land cannot meet minimum land reform requirements. It does nothing to address a growing Native population that requires a larger land base for community or sustainable development. For proper land reform, the settlement must identify the colonizers who are willing to sell their ill-gotten lands within our national territories. The US can buy out these willing sellers and return the purchased land to Native control and management. Purchasing fractionated land with settlement funds is the worst kind of fraud. It forces Native peoples to pay for what is theirs already. The colonizers walk away without any accountability for the conditions they created: poverty, land loss, ill health, substandard facilities, substandard education, and so forth.

No Provisions for Reparations

6. There is no provision in the settlement for the return of national land. Prior to the 1887 allotment act, the Oyate entered into several treaties with the Americans, namely, the Fort Laramie Treaty of 1851 and 1868. The 1868 Ft. Laramie Treaty recognized the Oyate's national boundaries. In that treaty, the Americans agreed to our demand that no cession of the Oyate's land is valid without the consent of three-fourths of the adult males. To this date, the Americans have *never* obtained the necessary supermajority because we have refused to cede our national lands. Not ceding our national lands, the Americans initiated a pogrom against the Oyate in 1876. This planned campaign of racism, persecution, and genocide has been the policy—despite the Americans' protestations to the contrary—ever since. These 1868 treaty-recognized lands eventually were subjected to the 1887 allotment act, which priva-

tized much of our national lands as individual trust allotments. The un-allotted lands were unilaterally declared "surplus" and sold to white settlers. Their descendants continue to illegally occupy our homeland. Affirming my nation's position, I say, return all our national lands to us that were stolen through the allotment act.

7. There is no provision in the settlement for stopping genocide. White President [Ulysses S.] Grant, along with other white administrators, issued an illegal 1876 order that labeled the Oyate as hostile against Americans. This order was nothing more than a ruse to justify American military action against my nation, the Oyate. The military defeat of the Americans, culminating in our victory at Greasy Grass [also known as the Battle of Little Bighorn, or Custer's Last Stand] in June 1876, led white Americans to increase their campaign of slaughtering millions and millions of buffalo. This campaign was a clear act of genocide since the buffalo provided for our nutrition and material well-being. By 1890, only 1,000 to 1,500 free roaming buffalo remained on the Plains. Their numbers have *never* recovered from the white American policy that nearly drove them to extinction. As a result, the decimation of buffalo left the Oyate without an adequate and healthy food source ever since. Today the Oyate suffer from disproportionate rates of diabetes and other health issues due directly to the forced change from a Native diet to a Western one.

The virtual elimination of the buffalo cleared the way for allotment. Forcing a farming lifestyle was one premise of allotment, and forcing dependence was another. Allotment promoted farming in a region that required massive, long-term, federal subsidies (e.g., irrigation, equipment, & maintenance), but Americans did not provide this support willingly. Six years before allotment, Helen Hunt Jackson wrote that American duplicity had all but destroyed my ancestors' sustainable way of life. Malnutrition and periods of starvation increased as

The *Cobell v. Salazar* Settlement Is Harmful to Its Class Members

There are multiple independent reasons to reject the [*Cobell v. Salazar*] settlement: the sprawling settlement administration class cannot be constitutionally certified; the parties have failed to quantify the value of dozens of claims being waived; the allocation of settlement proceeds bears no rational relationship to the alleged damages; the settlement makes many members of the mandatory class worse off than they were situated in the litigation; and the class representatives now have a conflict of interest with the rest of the class that makes them constitutionally inadequate representatives.

Furthermore, the settlement notice was materially misleading, and thus unconstitutional: It artificially discouraged many class members from opting out, though opting out would have been in their best interest. If the court is inclined to approve the settlement, it must require corrective notice and a new opportunity to opt out.

In the event that this court does approve the settlement, the fee and expense award for class counsel and the intervening attorneys, along with the class representative incentive payments (including "expenses"), should be capped at $50 million total.

Theodore H. Frank, on behalf of Kimberly Craven,
"Opposition of Kimberly Craven to Motion for Final Approval,"
Cobell v. Salazar, United States District Court
for the District of Columbia, June 20, 2011.

our major food source was systematically destroyed. Not coincidentally, allotment emerged as the panacea for problems that whites caused, but denied having inflicted. Allotment was an unprecedented, social engineering and culture modification program. Because of allotment's scale, it has destabilized my community ever since its imposition. Destabilization has taken many forms in our occupied land. . . . Colonization is an especially virulent form of genocide.

8. There is no provision in the settlement for apology for breach of trust. Since the 1887 allotment act, the Americans involved with "managing" our "trust" assets have an undeniable record of theft, lying, deceit, and greed, which has directly caused our impoverishment. Despite American protestations to the contrary, the allotment act's administration did not improve the well-being of the original allottees and their descendants. In 1881, six years before the allotment policy became law, Senator Henry Moore Teller from Colorado prophetically proclaimed that any allotment policy was little more than a white land grab clothed in Christian charitable rhetoric.

If I stand alone in the Senate, I want to put upon the record my prophecy in this matter, that when 30 or 40 years shall have passed and these Indians shall have parted with their title, they will curse the hand that was raised professedly in their defense to secure this kind of legislation, and if the people who are clamoring for it understood Indian character and Indian laws, and Indian morals, and Indian religion, they would not be here clamoring for this at all.

By the time allotting our national lands finally stopped in 1934, Native peoples' land base had diminished from approximately 140 million to about 50 million acres. Both Jackson and Teller laid bare their compatriots' greed-driven motivation six years before allotment became law. Their testimonies were well known, proving that Native interests were intentionally disregarded. Teller is right, of course; we do curse the hands that adopted this act and those who administer it.

No Provisions for Legally Protecting Native American Interests

9. There is no provision in the settlement terminating the plenary power doctrine. The settlement does nothing to end the Americans' doctrine of plenary power. This power was arbitrarily defined by the colonizers' court one year before the allotment act. This power is unilaterally invoked whenever Americans cannot defend a breach of their trust responsibilities to Native peoples. Were it not for the plenary power doctrine, the allotment act and other American human rights–violating laws would not have existed into the 21st century. Therefore, the doctrine reeks with the stench of colonization and its unrestrained abuse of power. The doctrine's continuance makes a complete mockery of any notion of American democracy, including the US Constitution.

10. There is no provision in the settlement recognizing treaty allotments. After June 1876, Americans experienced their first modern "9-11" when news of an American defeat reached the East. Americans reacted in anger toward my people and demanded that we cede the portion of our gold-producing homeland—the infamous sell or starve choice the Americans put to us. My ancestors refused to cede our national lands despite the Americans' threat to starve them. As a result, the Americans illegally annexed our land and nationalized them for the Americans. This act removed a substantial portion of our homelands from a treaty-recognized allotment scheme. Our Black Hills lands were stolen under a mere statute. Treaty allotments are not the same as allotments under the allotment act. They were not subject to alienation or US jurisdiction, as were those under the allotment act. Treaty allotments are held intact, beyond the reach of US statutes and therefore superior to statutory allotments. They have stronger protections than statutory allotments. Moreover, while the allotment act recognized treaty allotments, the administration of the allotment act did not adhere to the set acreages of the

treaty allotments—160 acres versus 320 acres. The allotment act violated other treaty provisions governing allotments. Inferior statutory allotments were used—illegally—to alienate yet more of our national lands. As a result, American colonizers who currently reside in our homeland are, in fact, illegal aliens.

11. There is no provision in the settlement to re-allocate forced-fee patent lands. In 1917, Indian Commissioner Cato Sells arbitrarily formulated a policy in which an allottee, who possessed less than one-half "Indian" blood, was unilaterally given a fee patent. This policy contravened treaty law regarding allotments, which required consent. All forced-fee patents originated from the 1887 allotment act. White colonizers obtained thousands of acreages through property tax deeds when our allottee ancestors could not pay taxes on these forced-fee patents. They did not know taxes were owed. Even if they knew, many were poor and could not afford to pay the taxes. The remedy to this colonizer scheme to steal land out from under our ancestors is to re-allocate to Native nations the equivalent in acreages that were lost due to the forced-fee patent policy.

12. There is no provision in the settlement to reimburse royalties that subsidized states. The allotment act specifically prohibits encumbering royalties from allotments. Yet, the 1962 *Running Horse et al. v. Udall* lawsuit showed that American officials were routinely—albeit illegally—approving state claims against individual Indian money (IIM) accounts for providing old-age assistance, aid to the blind, aid to the disabled, and aid to dependent children to allottees or their heirs prior to 1962. Any time allottees and their heirs left the reservation to shop, they paid state sales and other taxes on the goods and services purchased. Hence, they contributed to these state aid programs from the taxes paid. The settlement does not hold states liable for these encumbrances. Together, the states and the US colluded in a scheme to defraud Native people of their rightful royalties. This scheme is also called racketeering.

13. There is no provision in the settlement recognizing Native laws. This provision is further evidence of the Americans' willful intention to breach their trust responsibilities. The agreement is anti-Native sovereignty. It does not provide that the agreement shall be interpreted in accordance with the law of any particular Native nation. Native nations' laws and judicial systems are capable of interpreting the provisions of this settlement. Moreover, states are hostile to Native interests and cannot be trusted to impartially carry out the settlement's provisions that involve states. It is utterly inappropriate for the historic perpetrators of harms to name their own laws as the arbiters and executors of justice and to exclude any role for the sovereign laws and judicial and executive powers of those who suffered the harms.

> "Tribal gaming and tribal government spending supports thousands of jobs, creates millions of dollars in family income, and generates billions of dollars in economic activity."

Native American Casinos Benefit Both Tribal and Surrounding State and Local Economies

Barry Ryan

Barry Ryan is a policy analyst who specializes in public finance, economic development, and agriculture. In the following viewpoint, Ryan provides a detailed report on the tremendous economic and social advantages that tribal gaming and casinos bring to Minnesota, including in challenged rural areas. In addition to generating considerable income at the casinos themselves, the gaming industry supplies many full-time jobs with exceptional health and dental care insurance benefits. Ryan illustrates how these contributions, as well as the tribal gaming industry's investments in social spending and infrastructure, benefit all Minnesotans.

Barry Ryan, *The Economic Contributions of Minnesota Tribal Governments in 2007: A Study Commissioned by the Minnesota Indian Gaming Association,* Minnesota Indian Gaming Association, June 2009, pp. 2, 11–16. Reproduced by permission.

As you read, consider the following questions:

1. What percentage of the tribal gaming jobs were full time, according to Ryan?

2. How many of the more than six thousand Minnesota tribal government jobs were full time, according to the viewpoint?

3. How much did the tribal government spend on vendor goods and services within the rural Minnesota economy, according to Ryan?

This analysis examines the economic contributions to the Minnesota economy from tribal gaming and tribal government spending. It calculates the direct economic benefits of workforce spending, the secondary effects from spending on goods and services, plus the impacts of re-spending by workers, all of which support jobs and economic growth statewide. In addition to the central role tribal gaming plays in the Minnesota leisure and hospitality industry, the rural economy also gets a significant boost from the recycling of tribal gaming profits back into tribal government programs. Throughout the state, tribal gaming and tribal government spending supports thousands of jobs, creates millions of dollars in family income, and generates billions of dollars in economic activity. . . .

Tribal gaming: Minnesota tribal gaming directly supported 14,450 jobs in 2007, which represents 6% of the Minnesota leisure and hospitality industry (248,000 job) workforce. Tribal gaming had a total payroll of $411 million in 2007, equivalent to 11% of the entire leisure and hospitality industry's $3.9 billion payroll. In other words, the 6% of leisure and hospitality workers employed at tribal casino-resorts account for 11% of the industry payroll. Nearly all tribal casino-resort employees (96%) lived within the casino's local area economy and 27% of the tribal gaming workforce (3,900 employees) was Native

American. The 2007 tribal gaming workforce in rural Minnesota accounted for 10,675 jobs and a $273 million payroll.

Eighty percent or 11,600 tribal gaming jobs were full-time positions. Full-time workers enjoy a wide range of employer sponsored benefit programs, which typically take effect after 90 days of employment and a minimum 32-hour workweek. A study of the tribal gaming workforce in 2005 showed that casino-resort jobs are better jobs than the typical Minnesota leisure and hospitality industry job, and in many respects better jobs than the average Minnesota private sector employer.

Tribal Casinos Offer Premium Employee Benefits

Perhaps no employee benefit is more important to both the individual and their community than employer-supported health care. Tribal gaming employees in 2005 were more likely to be offered health care benefits, more likely to be enrolled in a plan, and more likely to have affordable medical and dental insurance coverage than the typical Minnesota leisure and hospitality worker. Tribal casino workers were also more likely to have access to flexible medical spending accounts than the average Minnesota private sector employee. In 2007, medical and dental insurance coverage for tribal gaming employees cost $67 million, including $54 million of spending in rural Minnesota.

The 2005 tribal casino workforce study documented a number of other benefit advantages of tribal gaming employment. Tribal casino workers had better access than the average Minnesota private sector employee to company-sponsored retirement savings plans and they put aside nearly $15 million in retirement savings in 2005 alone. They were also more likely to receive paid time off for holidays, vacations, and sick leave, a benefit worth $24 million. Tribal casino workers were also more likely to have life and disability insurance, and bet-

Total Economic Contributions from Minnesota Tribal Gaming and Government in 2007

	Rural Minnesota	Minnesota
Employment	30,525	41,700
Household Income	$882 million	$1.35 billion
Economic Output	$1.53 billion	$2.75 billion

TAKEN FROM: Barry Ryan, *The Economic Contributions of Minnesota Tribal Governments in 2007: A Study Commissioned by the Minnesota Gaming Association*, June 2009, p. 23.

ter access to educational assistance and flexible child care spending accounts than the typical Minnesota private sector employee.

Tribal governments: Minnesota tribal governments supported 6,100 jobs with a $165 million payroll in 2007. Two-thirds of tribal government workers or 4,000 jobs were full-time positions. The rural Minnesota tribal government workforce accounted for 5,400 jobs and a $147 million payroll. Among tribal government workers, 48% live on a reservation and 97% live within the local area economy. Tribal government workers enjoy the same employee benefits as tribal gaming workers. This means they too have many employer-sponsored benefits that exceed those of the average private sector employee. Tribal government employee medical and dental insurance coverage cost $23 million in 2007. Tribal government employee health care spending in rural Minnesota totaled $20 million.

Spending on Goods and Services

Tribal gaming purchases: Casino-resort vendor spending totaled $298 million statewide in 2007. Tribal casinos collectively had more than 10,000 vendor relationships, involving a wide range of goods and services from food products and utilities to advertising and other business services. Vendor spending in the rural Minnesota economy totaled $143 million. A second set of purchases were for construction, furnishings, equipment and other capital goods. Capital investments on tribal gaming enterprises totaled $257 million (based on three-year average annual spending between 2005 and 2007). Capital spending in the rural Minnesota economy totaled $109 million.

Although no two gaming enterprises are alike, the operating budget for a typical casino-resort can be divided into seven categories of goods and services. Marketing is the largest expense (28%), principally media advertising and other promotional activities. Food and beverage purchases for restaurants and other beverage service are the second largest expense (18%). The third biggest cost factor for the average casino-resort is facility maintenance spending (15%), including building repairs and grounds keeping. Electricity, water, and heating fuels accounted for 8% of operating costs. Resale items, such as motor fuels, tobacco products and retail merchandise are another 8% of total vendor purchases. Seven percent of expenditures are related to business services, such as accounting, financial, and legal services. A collection of other expenses, including everything from general administration to entertainer costs make up the remaining 16%.

Tribal government purchases: Tribal governments also made significant vendor spending and capital investment contributions to the Minnesota economy in 2007. Vendor spending on goods and services totaled $241 million statewide, including $125 million within the rural Minnesota economy. Although no two tribal governments are alike, the operating budget for a typical tribal government can be segmented into six spending categories. The largest expense (28%) is health care services for tribal members, including medical, dental, and vision care.

Tribal Investments in Social Programs and Infrastructure

The second biggest government operating expense is education (20%), ranging from day care and early childhood development programs to elementary, secondary, and postsecondary education spending, plus after-school programs and adult job training. Housing and economic development represents 13% of the typical tribal government budget, for programs such as housing assistance and small business loans. Human service expenditures, from family preservation, food assistance, and substance abuse programs to cultural and language programs, account for 10%. Another 7% goes to infrastructure operating costs, such as water, sewers, roads and other utility expenses. The remaining 22% covers a variety of services, such as public safety, natural resource management and general government administration.

Construction and other capital investments by tribal governments totaled $72 million statewide in 2007 (based on a three-year spending average). Capital spending in rural Minnesota totaled $29 million. Tribal governments have invested in a variety of capital projects, from building and improving roads, water, and waste treatment systems, to tribal facilities, like administrative office buildings, telecommunications centers, justice centers for courts and law enforcement, recreation and fitness centers, retirement centers for tribal elders, museums and libraries.

Health care: Health care spending is particularly important to rural areas of the state. Medical and dental care is not only essential to the individuals that are covered by employer sponsored plans, but a strong insured patient base helps create a viable health care system for those who lack such coverage. A strong health care network also increases the availability of emergency medical services, benefiting both local residents and the transient visitor. Minnesota tribes contribute to the viability of the rural health network by their significant direct spending on health care coverage for employees and tribal members. Medical and dental insurance coverage for tribal gaming employees and their families cost $67 million statewide in 2007. Coverage for rural Minnesota employees alone totaled $54 million. Health care benefits for tribal government workers cost $23 million statewide, including $20 million in rural Minnesota. Tribal governments spent an additional $57 million on medical and dental services for tribal members not covered by a family member working for the gaming division or the tribal government, and virtually all of this health care spending was in rural Minnesota. Collectively, health care spending by Minnesota tribes totaled $147 million in 2007. The rural Minnesota share was $130 million.

The total spending stimulus generated by tribal gaming and tribal government activities was $1.44 billion in 2007. Rural Minnesota captured 57% of this economic activity or $826 million in spending. The largest share of statewide spending was $576 million for tribal gaming and tribal government payrolls. The combined tribal workforce of 20,550 jobs included 15,600 full-time positions. In rural Minnesota the tribal payroll totaled $420 million, supporting 16,075 gaming and government jobs.

Vendor spending on tribal operations was $539 million statewide, including $268 million in rural Minnesota. Spending on construction and other capital investments totaled $329 million statewide and $138 million in rural Minnesota. This first round of spending on employee payrolls, vendor goods and services, and capital investments generated additional rounds of economic activity impacting nearly every sector of the state economy in 2007.

> "Today, alas, a political party votes bloc-
> like to keep its deep-pocketed
> benefactors' casino game as the only
> game in town."

Tribal-Owned Casinos Take Money Away from State and Local Economies

Gary Larson

*Gary Larson is a retired magazine editor and conservative jour-
nalist who lives in Minnesota. In the following viewpoint, Larson
strongly objects to what he characterizes as an unfair Native
American monopoly on gaming in Minnesota and decries an
editorial written by John McCarthy in response to an earlier editorial by Larson that supported the approval of racinos, or casinos at racetracks, in Minnesota. Larson condemns McCarthy's
editorial as unfair, unethical, and indicative of the highly partisan approach to gaming in Minnesota, whereby wealthy tribal
casino backers fund liberal politicians who then ensure that no
legislation is passed that would allow the establishment of gaming enterprises owned by non–Native Americans. Larson claims
that McCarthy paints him as a racist in an attempt to disguise*

Gary Larson, "Protecting the Native American Casino Monopoly in Minnesota," *Intellectual Conservative*, June 3, 2011. Reproduced by permission of the author.

the discrimination against non–Native American–owned gaming initiatives that liberal Minnesota politicians support on behalf of Native American casinos.

As you read, consider the following questions:

1. What percentage of Minnesota residents are in favor of racinos, according to Larson?

2. According to Larson, what is John McCarthy's occupation?

3. What is the total estimated annual operating profit of Native American casino operations in Minnesota, according to Larson?

An abhorrent "counterpoint" in the [Minnesota] *StarTribune*, Minneapolis's mainstream daily, by a longtime Minnesota casino lobbyist, is the very definition of demagoguery [distorting reality by playing on emotion]. Lobbyist John McCarthy's *ad hominem* [discrediting the person making the argument rather than the substance of the argument] attack on me, personally, while distorting the history of racino [casinos at racetracks] legislation at the legislature, is emblematic proof of wretched excesses and loony tunes arguments surrounding an issue of putting "slot gaming" at the state's two racetracks.

Why the *StarTribune* ran his heedless, reckless collapse of judgment, contrary to known facts, and potentially libelously, is somewhat of a mystery. McCarthy's nasty, jagged-edged May 4 [2011] piece is called a "counterpoint" to my straight-on op-ed, "Indian casino lobby and the DFL [Democratic-Farmer-Labor] party it props up" (April 30 [2011]) in the same newspaper. My commentary favors the state legislature approving, after a half dozen tries, enabling "racino" legislation, breaking up a known de facto monopoly.

Racinos are relatively new, a hybrid of casino-style gambling, such as "slot gaming," at racetracks, both doggie and horse genre. Twelve states now permit racinos, including New York and Pennsylvania, supporting larger purses (prizes) for horse racing, in some cases rescuing tracks from financial doom, thereby saving tens of thousands of jobs and paying taxes, too. (In Pennsylvania, three-quarters of a *billion* dollars in taxes in 2009 alone were paid by racinos, while saving something like 5,200 jobs at that state's racetracks.)

A Clear Bias in Favor of Tribal Casinos

The casino lobbyist's "counterpoint," titled "Column put the 'race' in racino proposal" (May 4), is a cheap hit job. It reeks of willful, self-serving historical error, purporting for example, a notion that bipartisan action at the legislature at the Capitol in St. Paul killed previous attempts to gain approval for racinos.

Bipartisan? Not by a long shot. Democrats in Minnesota— here called DFLers, a strange amalgam of Democrat and Farmer-Labor Parties fashioned out of political expediency by Hubert H. Humphrey in the mid-forties—put up every road-block to racinos. They killed every bill to permit racetracks, or anyone else, such as the Mall of America, from having one-armed bandits [slot machines], the most popular form of public gambling, according to the American Gaming Association.

Slots elsewhere, you see, would be competition—thus, anathema—for the DFLers' deep-pocketed campaign benefactors—the indigenous, now fantastically wealthy tribes that own and operate 18 casinos in this lovely Land of 10,000-plus Lakes. (Disclosure: Admitted bias here, it is my place of birth and my summer homeland.)

Sovereign, tribal-run enterprises, all reservation-based, they rely on the generosity of not strangers, but friends in the legislature, mostly staunch DFL majorities through the years, to defeat any like competition for their casinos. Newly enfran-

"Indian Affairs Then and Now," cartoon by Monte Wolverton, www.CagleCartoons.com.
Copyright © 2006 by Monte Wolverton and www.CagleCartoons.com.

chised, now heavy-hitters at the lobbying game, Sioux tribes
and Objibe bands constitute a *de facto* [in practice] monopoly
in Minnesota. It amounts to corruption of a high order, right
under the noses of snoozing, curiously incurious news media.
Silence of the liberal classes? Sticking together?

Casinos here enjoy enormous, untaxed profits on their
gambling proceeds, money tapped liberally, like a big-teated
cash cow, for DFLers' political campaigns. That is indisputable
fact, as reported to the state in campaign finance records. It is
non-news, though, buried in news reports that purport to tell
the story of campaign financing. (Shhhh!)

(Casino interests in Minnesota are second only to the
teachers' union in gift-giving to the DFL. In some years casino-
rich tribes rank #1 in giving to their DFL allies. This year,
2011, to stem the rising public tide—70 percent!—in favor of
racinos, 40 or more lobbyists did the tribes' bidding at the
legislature. Cost is no object, and lawyer-lobbyists are known
to be expensive creatures.)

A Shamefully False and Irresponsible Attack on Dissenting Opinion

Calling me "an old Indian fighter," as McCarthy does, is a cheap shot, even figuratively untrue. For some unfathomable reason he labels my *StarTribune* op-ed ". . . hate speech against native Americans." Huh? Recklessly untrue, likely laced with malice aforethought, his remark embraces all the earmarks of libel if one pursued the obvious. It would be, of course, a Pyrrhic victory [a victory that comes at great cost to the victor] (*New York Times Co. v. Sullivan*, 1964).

Put simply, he plays the race card. Yes, indeed, it IS the last refuge of scoundrels, *à la* O.J. Simpson's criminal trial. By flinging rhetorical mud balls, and dissembling known reality, he evidently has something to fear, and zero regard for civil discourse or rational discussion. Vile name-calling will do in a storm? Can't debate issues? Then turn to vitriol.

What prompts a newspaper, even a traditionally "liberal" sheet such as the *StarTribune*, to publish such a vile "counterpoint" (quotation marks mine) that labels me bigot? A spewer of "hate speech" toward a minority population? Theories, anyone?

Independent surveys confirm 70 percent of Minnesotans want a racino in their midst, whether they'd patronize one, or not. Does that make 70 percent of the state "old Indian fighters"? Does a predisposition to favor a little competition in the state's gambling mix amount to "hate speech against native Americans"?

Nah. Don't be silly. It is the mark of transparent demagoguery.

The shopworn tactic of labeling all who disagree with you as bigots, even hate-mongers, is flung about with disgusting frequency nowadays. It is repeated unabashedly, almost cheerfully, by demagogues' camp followers including, sadly, "the press." It's all rather pathetic.

Name-caller McCarthy's day job is executive director of the Minnesota Indian Gaming Association (MIGA). On the side, he is a fund-raiser for his party's DFL candidates, serving no less as their campaign managers in a remote "Upnorth" place named Bemidji [a city in northern Minnesota].

Why are we not surprised by his dual role as lead casino lobbyist and DFL fund-raiser? Okay, so wild-eyed partisan hyperbole is to be expected from a hired gun, a loose cannon. But spreading blatant lies? Name-calling? Not even black-hatted Jack Abramoff [former casino lobbyist convicted of mail fraud and conspiracy] did that while spreading casino booty to both sides of the aisle, and running afoul of the law.

McCarthy's smarmy pitch, dutifully picked up by toady news media, is that racinos at racetracks would somehow "expand gambling." Ah ha! At least since colonial days, patrons have flocked to racetracks to gamble, yes, not only to watch ponies run. Fancy *that*! Gambling, at a *gambling* venue! What's next? Beer in beer joints?

So much to criticize, starting with the headline, "Column put the 'race' in racino proposal." My op-ed did no such thing. The newspaper's unattributed headline is, quite simply, a lie. But then, headlines sometimes do that, leading readers astray from facts and other worthy notions, like simple truths, especially when agendas are to be pushed.

In his text, McCarthy strays inexplicably to an event about 150 years ago, "the hanging of 38 Sioux warriors at Mankato [Minnesota]." Stated as if it had something to do with today's anti-racino legislative battles, the event was federal prosecution during the [Abraham] Lincoln administration that convicted warpath Indians for murdering and in some cases, also raping and scalping, hundreds of settlers on the frontier.

What in blazes does that have to do with the racinos? Well, nothing. Really! Citing the 150-year-old case to fulminate against racinos is the mark of demagoguery, illogical, a *non sequitur* [a remark that has nothing to do with the subject at hand] of the worst kind. McCarthy claims a "state statute" and an early Minnesota governor sought out the Sioux warriors. Not true. It was an order of the U.S. Army to hunt down and prosecute marauding warriors for heinous crimes against hundreds of white settlers. Heck, McCarthy could even look it up in the history books.

So today, alas, a political party votes bloc-like to keep its deep-pocketed benefactors' casino game as the only game in town. Some dare call a spade what it is, that the DFL is "slave" to its Indian paymasters, allowing for a bit of euphemistic fervor here. To a former Republican minority leader, Senator Dick Day (R-Owatonna), the DFL is "a wholly owned subsidiary of the tribal casinos." *Touche!*

In 2010, Minnesota casino-rich tribes thrust $1.3 million into DFL candidates' hands, according to state records. In the election cycle before that, during which a public smoking ban was exempted for Indian casinos, tribal interests tossed $1.2 million into state DFL pals' campaigns. Hey, money talks! Walks, too.

Quid pro quo, anyone? Just coincidence? Sure, pigs soar. And hell freezeth over.

Native Americans Should Not Have Exclusive "Rights" to Gaming

At one time a DFL Senate majority leader uproariously claimed "slot gaming" exclusively at Indian casinos was an "Indian gaming right." As if God-given; written in the stars. You had to be a Believer. In an Orwellian twist, the DFL chieftain gave new meaning to entitlement—that a casino monopoly is racially bestowed, of all things. Fan-tastic!

The oft-repeated mantra "gaming rights" evolved to a new rallying cry—that granting such "rights" to anyone except in-state tribes, would be (get this!) "expansion of gambling." Ironically, Indian casinos did all the expanding—from four casinos in the 1990s, to 18 at present. None of this was reported or opined about by incurious news media, hysterical now about "expansion" only at two tax-paying racetracks. (The state's tax take? About $250 million every biennium, that's all.)

Labeling competition for its sugar daddies "expansion" is *de rigueur* [fashionable necessity] for the political left here, protecting their collective asses—er, their campaign coffers. Their allies in media recite the "expansion" line as Gospel. No one rocks the boat. All media observe the emperor's new clothes. Theirs is today's journalistic hubris that says, we report what we select and spin it the way we like, and truth can just go to hell.

Thus is a safety net spread over the *de facto* casino monopoly in Minnesota.

Paying off a political party for protecting one's turf is a forever thing here in the Gopher State. State-tribal compacts, negotiated (if that is the right word) by the give-away-the-store DFL administration in 1989, have no expiration dates. No sunsetting. They just keep giving and giving, outlasting even a fully charged Energizer bunny.

"For people like Gary Larson," McCarthy concludes in his gutter-level hit piece, "it's a win-win-win when Indians lose." (Note: ". . . people like"?) His presumption that "slot gaming" at two little racetracks near the Twin Cities threaten a thriving empire of well-established, close-to-home Indian casinos, is bogus. His Indian casino clients have an estimated operating profit—after paying prizes—of $1.4 billion annually. They spend untold millions in advertising, whatever that fact might, or might not, imply. I only raise the issue.

Intellectual honesty and historical integrity are not in McCarthy's bag, nor in media's non-reporting. Unapologetic editorial page staffers who ran his lie-laced claptrap (sorry, no other word fits) ought to be ashamed. Free-flowing, uninhibited but civil discourse on public issues is one thing, yes, but smearing and spreading utter falsehoods? I don't think so.

Say you, then, libertarian reader, "all's fair in love, war and politics"? Think again. Where a political party trumps all competition on behalf of its cash-rich untaxed benefactors, nothing less than institutional corruption is at hand. All told, one more reason a cynical public is turned off by politicians' double-dealing, ranking them—along with lawyers, near the bottom of the ethical heap, and journalists. As formerly one of the latter, a one-time reporter and editor, I can only say— OUCH!

"Poverty is both the cause and the consequence of all the ills visited upon Native Americans. Failure to address poverty causes deprivation and hardship in these communities today, and robs the next generation of any opportunity to succeed and thrive tomorrow."

Additional Government Assistance Is Urgently Needed to Address Native American Poverty

Tom Rodgers

Tom Rodgers is the president of Carlyle Consulting in Alexandria, Virginia, and a member of the Blackfeet tribe who advocates on behalf of Native American tribal governments. In the following viewpoint, Rodgers declares that the living conditions in Native American communities are desperate and that the US government needs to not only make good on its past promises to Native Americans but also direct more attention, funding, and targeted legislation to address their plight. Rodgers argues that mistreatment of Native Americans by the US government has

Tom Rodgers, "Native American Poverty," *Spotlight on Poverty and Opportunity*, December 10, 2008. Reproduced by permission.

been a part of the twentieth and twenty-first centuries, even though the outright violence and neglect of earlier centuries has passed. The author cites alarming statistics to convey the dire state in which Native Americans are forced to live and to dispel the myth that most tribes have great wealth from gaming operations. Rodgers outlines what he thinks needs to happen to save Native American communities from devastation: more aggressive government attention to policies dealing with Native Americans and swifter action on funding initiatives that are already in place, especially in the area of health care. Rodgers expresses hope that the administration of President Barack Obama will provide greater assistance for Native Americans than past administrations.

As you read, consider the following questions:

1. What sparked the Dakota War of 1862 between the Dakota Sioux Indians and the US government, according to the viewpoint?

2. What percentage of males in high-poverty Native American communities are employed full-time and year-round, according to Rodgers?

3. In what year was the Indian Health Care Improvement Act first passed, and what was its purpose, according to the viewpoint?

> To be a poor man is hard, but to be a poor race in a land of dollars is the very bottom of hardships.
>
> —*W.E.B. DuBois*

No discussion of poverty, and of the need to renew opporNtunity in America, can be complete without a frank consideration of the situation faced by Native Americans. With a worsening economy, the inevitable churn of holiday stories about the least fortunate, and a new administration [referring to the start of the Barack Obama administration in January

2009], now is the right time for meaningful action to address poverty in Native American communities.

The modern history of Native Americans has been marred by tragedy and injustice, and too often deprivation and suffering within Native American communities have been met with sentiment that shocks the conscience.

In 1862, the American government refused to honor treaty obligations to the Dakota Sioux Indians during a time of widespread starvation. When tribal leaders, desperate for relief, asked for food on credit because the U.S. government had failed to provide moneys owed, an associate of the local Indian agent replied, "If they are hungry, let them eat grass or their own dung." His comment, and the crass disregard it represented, helped to spark the infamous and bloody confrontation between the tribe and the federal government now known as the Dakota War.

Staggering Statistics on Native American Poverty

Although we have moved beyond wanton neglect and violence, our national response to the problem of poverty in Native American communities remains woefully inadequate.

The extent of the problem may not be well known. American Indians and Native Alaskans number 4.5 million. According to the U.S. Census Bureau, these Americans earn a median annual income of $33,627. One in every four (25.3 percent) lives in poverty and nearly a third (29.9 percent) are without health insurance coverage.

To put this in stark terms, counties on Native American reservations are among the poorest in the country and, according to the Economic Research Service at the U.S. Department of Agriculture, nearly 60 percent of all Native Americans who live outside of metropolitan areas inhabit persistently poor counties.

Contrary to popular belief, the overwhelming majority of tribes are not wealthy by virtue of gaming. This is mostly attributable to a fact which all sovereign nations have come to understand, that geography is all too often destiny.

For most tribes, their remotely placed homes and communities frequently stifle viable economic activity. This disturbing result is particularly harsh when we recognize that Native Americans witnessed their geography chosen for them by those who sought to terminate them as a people.

A major cause of poverty in Native American communities is the persistent lack of opportunity. The Economic Research Service reports that Native American communities have fewer full-time employed individuals than any other high-poverty community. Only 36 percent of males in high-poverty Native American communities have full-time, year-round employment.

On the Blackfeet reservation in Montana, for example, the annual unemployment rate is 69 percent. The national unemployment rate at the very peak of the Great Depression was around 25 percent. That means that each year the Blackfeet people, whose aboriginal lands once comprised Glacier National Park, suffers an employment crisis nearly three times as severe as the Great Depression.

One does not need to travel to a developing nation to find extreme poverty. It is here, in America. In our own backyard.

Support for Basic Services Is Greatly Needed

Yet beyond these bleak statistics, there is very little discussion of the causes of Native American poverty and what to do about it. The sad truth is only a handful of policy makers give Native Americans priority on the national agenda. Few even know that November was Native American Heritage Month and that, by congressional resolution, the Friday after Thanksgiving is Native American Heritage Day.

US Unemployment Rate from 1997 to 2007

Year	White	American Indian/Alaska Native	Black
1997	4.2	10.8	10.9
1998	4.0	10.1	9.3
1999	3.5	11.9	8.4
2000	3.4	9.7	7.6
2001	3.6	10.6	8.8
2002	5.1	13.1	10.9
2003	5.2	14.5	11.3
2004	5.1	10.4	10.7
2005	4.5	12.3	10.8
2006	4.1	7.3	10.1
2007	4.0	11.9	8.2

TAKEN FROM: Jonathan Mooney, *Tribes, Energy and Economic Independence: Barriers and Opportunities*, Prepared for Environmental Finance Center Region IX, Dominican University of California, San Rafael, November 2010, p. 3.

In a time for giving thanks, we too readily forget that one of the first stories behind Thanksgiving dates to 1621, when it is said to have been celebrated by the pilgrims at Plymouth and the Wampanoag tribe of Massachusetts.

In addition to their symbolic exclusion from the table, America's indigenous populations have struggled for recognition. Most of the world's nations have been reluctant to take positive steps to support the rights of indigenous peoples. The United Nations Permanent Forum on Indigenous [Issues] set a goal early this century for adoption of the Declaration on the Rights of Indigenous Peoples. In 2007, 143 countries finally adopted the declaration. The United States—the wealthiest country in the world—was not one of them.

Expanding formal rights is important, but we also need better federal performance on these issues. The Government

Accountability Office (GAO) has leveled a number of criticisms at the agencies responsible for federal Native American policy, including "long-standing financial and programmatic deficiencies" in the Interior Department's American Indian programs. A 2006 GAO report also found that the Office of the Special Trustee for American Indians has failed to implement several key initiatives specified by the American Indian Trust Fund Management Reform Act of 1994, including establishing an actual timetable for completing its mission.

The government should also take more aggressive action on providing essential services and the necessary tools for effective self-governance to Native American communities. Congress has failed to reauthorize the Indian Health Care Improvement Act since 1992. Initially passed in 1976, the Indian Health Care Improvement Act was designed to bring the waning health of Native American communities up to the standard enjoyed by all Americans.

Unfortunately, current inaction on this issue constitutes a grave travesty. Health systems in many Native American communities are in serious need of updating and improvement. Reauthorizing this legislation will improve disease screening in Native American communities, encourage health enrollment in existing federal programs, provide better investment in Native American health professionals, and ensure funding in order to modernize facilities in Native American communities.

If providing better health care to Native Americans during a time of Wall Street bailouts seems too costly, we should recognize that we currently spend 30 percent more per capita on health care in American prisons than on Native Americans, whose ancestors aided the Pilgrims, fed the soldiers freezing in Valley Forge, helped Lewis and Clark explore our nation, and proudly hoisted the flag on Iwo Jima. In fact, Native Americans most recently served their country by playing the first and leading role in exposing one of the largest congressional corruption scandals in history: the Jack Abramoff scandal.

Awareness, Recognition, and Aid Must Increase

The truth is that health care is merely one example of the way we consistently deprive Native American communities of the services they desperately need. A 2003 study by the U.S. Commission on Civil Rights found that, per capita, Native Americans receive disproportionately lower funding than the general population for federally administered services and programs. This means that for every essential service our government agrees to provide for its citizens—including basic law enforcement, education, and infrastructure—Native Americans get less than any other segment of society.

The time for action is long past due. Native Americans were the very last to be granted the right to vote, and were therefore too long treated as second-class citizens. Now there are those who seek to treat Native American governments as second-class sovereigns. They seek to accomplish this by not availing them of the same tools for self-reliance and recognition afforded to state and local governments.

The issue of poverty is an integral first step. Poverty is both the cause and the consequence of all the ills visited upon Native Americans. Failure to address poverty causes deprivation and hardship in these communities today, and robs the next generation of any opportunity to succeed and thrive tomorrow.

The invisibility, silence, and neglect must end. As President-elect Barack Obama ascends to the White House, now is the significant moment to address the many problems Native Americans endure, including systemic poverty.

Barack Obama's election symbolizes America's progress in healing the racial wounds that scar our history. A new commitment to Native Americans will continue that process. His pledge to reduce poverty in America should extend to the Native American communities that feel poverty most acutely and that have been relegated to the shadows of our society for far too long.

Advocates, legislators, and the new president must put Native Americans on the national agenda. Including Native Americans in our vision of a better America is an indispensable part of the "change we need."

> *"Yes, the government signed treaties with the tribes that make Indians 'special.' But that 'specialness' has brought the Indians socialism. It's what keeps them dependent and poor."*

US Government Assistance Has Generated Native American Poverty

John Stossel

John Stossel is a journalist and television commentator who hosts the program Stossel *on the Fox Business Network. He is the author of* Give Me a Break *and* Myths, Lies and Downright Stupidity. *In the following viewpoint, Stossel argues that the US government's assistance to Native Americans has created their poverty. To support his contention, Stossel points to the prosperous Lumbee tribe in North Carolina that is not federally recognized as a sovereign nation and thus does not receive any US government assistance. It is precisely because the Lumbees are free from the burden of government support, Stossel maintains, that they are free from the socialist mentality that burdens Native Americans living on reservations. The Lumbees are creative, productive, resourceful, and financially successful because they*

John Stossel, "Government Creates Poverty," April 27, 2011. Reproduced by permission of John Stossel and Creators Syndicate, Inc.

know that they cannot depend on government handouts. Stossel disparages efforts to recognize the Lumbees as a sovereign nation and make them eligible for federal funds because, he declares, changing their focus from fostering entrepreneurship to fostering a bureaucratic and dependent mind-set would destroy the prosperity they have enjoyed for years.

As you read, consider the following questions:

1. What is the poverty rate among Native Americans, according to the viewpoint?

2. How much federal funding would the Lumbee tribe receive under the Lumbee Recognition Act, according to Stossel?

3. What was the title of Stossel's controversial television special, which he claims prompted "predictable vitriol" from viewers?

The U.S. government has "helped" no group more than it has "helped" the American Indians. It stuns me when President [Barack] Obama appears before Indian groups and says things like, "Few have been ignored by Washington for as long as Native Americans."

Ignored? Are you kidding me? They should be so lucky. The government has made most Indian tribes wards of the state. Government manages their land, provides their health care, and pays for housing and child care. Twenty different departments and agencies have special "Native American" programs. The result? Indians have the highest poverty rate, nearly 25 percent, and the lowest life expectancy of any group in America. Sixty-six percent are born to single mothers.

Nevertheless, Indian activists want more government "help."

It is intuitive to assume that, when people struggle, government "help" is the answer. The opposite is true. American groups who are helped the most do the worst.

The Lumbees Succeed Because They Receive No "Help"

Consider the Lumbees of Robeson County, N.C.—a tribe not recognized as sovereign by the government and therefore ineligible for most of the "help" given other tribes. The Lumbees do much better than those recognized tribes.

Lumbees own their homes and succeed in business. They include real estate developer Jim Thomas, who used to own the Sacramento Kings, and Jack Lowery, who helped start the Cracker Barrel restaurants. Lumbees started the first Indian-owned bank, which now has 12 branches.

The Lumbees' wealth is not from casino money.

"We don't have any casinos. We have 12 banks," says Ben Chavis, another successful Lumbee businessman. He also points out that Robeson County looks different from most Indian reservations.

"There's mansions. They look like English manors. I can take you to one neighborhood where my people are from and show you nicer homes than the whole Sioux reservation."

Despite this success, professional "victims" activists want Congress to make the Lumbees dependent—like other tribes. U.S. Rep. Mike McIntyre, D-N.C., has introduced the Lumbee Recognition Act, which would give the Lumbees the same "help" other tribes get—about $80 million a year. Some members of the tribe support the bill.

Of course they do.

People like to freeload.

Lawyer Elizabeth Homer, who used to be the U.S. Interior Department's director of Indian land trusts, says the Lumbees ought to get federal recognition.

"The Lumbees have been neglected and left out of the system, and have been petitioning for 100 years. . . . They're entitled, by the way."

Socialism Has Been the Downfall of Native Americans

Socialism will destroy America the same way it has destroyed the American Indian. If we are going to learn anything from the tribes and nations, it should be that the experiment has failed.

American Indian Tea Party Nation,
"One Big Reservation," July 20, 2010.
http://americanindianteapartynation.wordpress.com.

People like Homer will never get it. Lumbees do well because they've divorced themselves from government handouts. Washington's neglect was a godsend.

Government Aid Leads to Welfare and Socialism

Some Lumbees don't want the handout.

"We shouldn't take it!" Chavis said. He says if federal money comes, members of his tribe "are going to become welfare cases. It's going to stifle creativity. On the reservations, they haven't trained to be capitalists. They've been trained to be communists."

Tribal governments and the Bureau of Indian Affairs manage most Indian land. Indians compete to serve on tribal councils because they can give out the government's money. Instead of seeking to become entrepreneurs, members of tribes aspire to become bureaucrats.

"You can help your girlfriend; you can help your girlfriend's mama. It's a great program!" Chavis said sarcastically.

Because a government trust controls most Indian property, individuals rarely build nice homes or businesses. "No individual on the reservation owns the land. So they can't develop it," Chavis added. "Look at my tribe. We have titles and deeds to our land. That's the secret. I raise cattle. I can do what I want to because it's my private property."

I did a TV segment on the Lumbees that I included in a special called "Freeloaders." That won me the predictable vitriol. Apparently, I'm ignorant of history and a racist.

The criticism misses the point. Yes, many years ago white people stole the Indians' land and caused great misery. And yes, the government signed treaties with the tribes that make Indians "special." But that "specialness" has brought the Indians socialism. It's what keeps them dependent and poor.

On the other hand, because the U.S. government never signed a treaty with the Lumbees, they aren't so "special" in its eyes. That left them mostly free.

Freedom lets them prosper.

Periodical and Internet Sources Bibliography

The following articles have been selected to supplement the diverse views presented in this chapter.

Simon Akam	"Old Wound, Same Pain," *New Statesman*, June 11, 2009.
Noah Bierman	"Casino Provision for Tribe Sparks Debate," *Boston Globe*, August 26, 2011.
Julie Delcour	"Cobell v. Salazar: Riding into the Calvary and Surviving," *Tulsa World*, December 13, 2009.
D. Michael McBride, Anthony Broadman, and Jack Duran	"Legal Panel: More Legal Challenges Ahead for Tribes in 2011," *Indian Gaming*, January 2011.
Ojibwa	"The War on Poverty," Native American Netroots, August 17, 2011. http://native americannetroots.net.
S.E. Ruckman	"Cobell Settlement: So Close, Yet So Far," *Native American Times*, August 10, 2010. http://nativetimes.com.
Katia Savchuk	"Massive Digital Divide for Native Americans Is 'A Travesty,'" PBS.org, May 12, 2011. www .pbs.org.
Scott Scanlon	"Urban Casinos—Parting Thoughts," *Niagara Views* (blog), August 29, 2011. http://blogs .buffalonews.com.
Kelley Weiss	"Tribal Rights Hinder Child Support for Mothers," NPR.org, August 13, 2011. www.npr.org.
Julia Whitty	"Elouise Cobell's Bittersweet Victory," *Mother Jones*, December 8, 2009.

For Further Discussion

Chapter 1

1. How convincing do you find John Hayward's contention that there was no possible way that the US military meant any offense to Geronimo's descendants or to Native Americans? Does he provide evidence to back up his claim that the military's use of Native American tribal names and culture in naming their weapons systems is an honor? Do you find the similarities and differences between Karl Jacoby's and Hayward's accounts of Geronimo's life story significant in terms of how they contribute to their arguments? Why or why not? Do you think that Jacoby's claim that Americans know little to nothing about the Indian rights movement and other important aspects of Native American history is valid? Why or why not? If he does have a valid point, then does this explain why Native American names and icons continue to be used by the US military?

2. Both Tex G. Hall and Rain Smith express concern for how team mascots affect the way young people view Native Americans in general and themselves in particular. In Smith's viewpoint, Chief Lee Vest recalls fondly his high school's team mascot, the Native American warrior, and says that the "Warrior Spirit" inspired and energized him. Vest also adds that the term "redskins" should never be used because it is highly offensive and denotes a tragic history. Hall's viewpoint indicates that any use of Native American images and names as team mascots demeans and objectifies Native Americans and perpetuates inaccurate and often offensive stereotypes. Do you think that distinctions can be made in the minds of young people

between Native American–themed mascots that are meant to honor Native Americans and those that are offensive? If so, then on what do you think those distinctions are based? And if not, then who, if anyone, can or should make those distinctions? Would it be better to simply eliminate the use of Native American–themed mascots? Why or why not?

Chapter 2

1. Which problems with the tribal justice and public safety programs outlined by Theresa M. Pouley are addressed in the Government Accountability Office (GAO) report? Which problems are not addressed? Given the evidence presented by the GAO, do you feel that its optimism is warranted? Why or why not?

2. Zach Einterz and Carl Horowitz advocate dismantling the Bureau of Indian Affairs (BIA) because of widespread, deeply ingrained corruption, but each offers a very different perspective on who is corrupt, what led to the current state of affairs as he sees it, and what the best alternatives are for Native Americans going forward. Based on Lisa Shellenberger's commentary about the function of the BIA, consider what the consequences might be if either Horowitz's or Einterz's recommendations were implemented. How would the two scenarios be similar? How would they differ?

Chapter 3

1. Janet Roberson asserts that Glen Cove has been "desecrated . . . by vandals who have defaced the site with extensive graffiti declaring 'sacred burial ground' (often misspelled) and other similar phrases." She also refers to "activists who have set up camp in the area" who "have erected unpermitted portable restrooms in close proximity to where the small permanent restroom is planned, show-

ing that even those who claim they are offended by the planned restrooms need them and have put porta-potties over land they have labeled as sacred." Do you feel that these references to "vandals" and "activists" support or undermine the effectiveness of Roberson's argument? Is the fact that Roberson fails to identify herself as a former board member of the Greater Vallejo Recreation District and instead claims to represent one of many individuals "who live next to the land and have taken great interest in this issue" significant? Why or why not? Is the tone of the Roberson viewpoint similar to or different from the tone of the viewpoint presented by the Sacred Sites Protection and Rights of Indigenous Tribes (SSP&RIT)? Which viewpoint is more persuasive? Why?

Chapter 4

1. Elouise P. Cobell admits that the amount of the *Cobell v. Salazar* settlement is far less than the total owed to Native Americans by the US government, yet maintains that the fact that it is the largest settlement ever awarded to Native Americans is a cause for celebration, and the fact that the desperately needed funds will help to address the suffering of impoverished Native Americans in the immediate future is a compelling reason to settle rather than continue to fight for more money. Cobell acknowledges that there is opposition to the settlement among Native Americans, but she argues that these objections are based on misunderstandings about the agreed-upon terms. Edward Charles Valandra vehemently opposes the settlement and determines that it is not only inadequate and insulting but also dangerous to Native Americans. What makes each of their arguments more or less convincing? Can you detect any common ground between the two? If so, what might that be?

2. How well does John Stossel support his contention that
   government aid is the cause of the exceptionally high poverty rate among Native Americans? Does his use of terms
   such as "freeloader" and phrases such as "professional
   'victims' activists" help or harm his credibility? Does he
   offer sufficient examples to refute statistics offered by Tom
   Rodgers that suggest that poverty among Native Americans is due to insufficient funding of service programs
   rather than to excess government aid?

Organizations to Contact

The editors have compiled the following list of organizations concerned with the issues debated in this book. The descriptions are derived from materials provided by the organizations. All have publications or information available for interested readers. The list was compiled on the date of publication of the present volume; the information provided here may change. Be aware that many organizations take several weeks or longer to respond to inquiries, so allow as much time as possible.

Administration for Native Americans (ANA)
370 L'Enfant Promenade SW
2nd Floor West Aerospace Center
Washington, DC   20447-0002
(877) 922-9262
e-mail: anacomments@acf.hhs.gov
website: www.acf.hhs.gov/programs/ana

The Administration for Native Americans (ANA) is a federal organization working to promote economic and social self-sufficiency for all Native Americans. The ANA invests in community-based projects focused on social and economic development, language preservation, and environmental regulatory enhancement. It publishes materials related to these projects on its website.

American Civil Liberties Union (ACLU)
125 Broad Street, 18th Floor, New York, NY   10004-2400
(212) 549-2500
website: www.aclu.org

The American Civil Liberties Union (ACLU) is a national organization that works to defend the civil rights guaranteed by the US Constitution. Its members believe that it is essential to be informed of one's rights in order to be able to exercise them. The ACLU publishes and distributes policy statements, pamphlets, the semiannual newsletter *Civil Liberties Alert*, and several books including *The Rights of the Indians and Tribes: The Basic ACLU Guide to Indian and Tribal Rights.*

American Indian Environmental Office (AIEO)

1200 Pennsylvania Avenue NW, Washington, DC   20460
(202) 564-0303
e-mail: tribal.portal@epa.gov
website: www.epa.gov/indian

The American Indian Environmental Office (AIEO) is part of the federal Environmental Protection Agency (EPA) and focuses on helping Native American tribes administer their own environmental programs. The AIEO publishes a newsletter, *The American Indian Tribal Portal*, which is available on its website and contains a wealth of information on environmental laws and regulations, environmental tribal policies, and other environmental media data.

American Indian Heritage Foundation (AIHF)

PO Box 6301, Falls Church, VA   22040
(703) 819-0979
e-mail: palemoon@indians.org
website: www.indians.org

The American Indian Heritage Foundation (AIHF) is a nonprofit organization that was established to provide relief services to Native Americans and to build bridges of understanding between natives and non–Native Americans. AIHF programs include an emergency relief distribution program, scholarship program, and student award program. The AIHF website contains an exhaustive tribal directory and a large collection of indigenous peoples' literature.

American Indian Tea Party Nation

website: http://americanindianteapartynation.wordpress.com

The American Indian Tea Party Nation is a nonpartisan, intertribal online group with the stated goal of exposing corruption in both the Democratic and Republican Parties. The group began as Native Americans Against Obama but later expanded to include members with similar beliefs in smaller government and lower taxes. The categories listed on the group's blog include Anti-Congress, Anti-Obama, Health Care, History, Issues, Media, Poverty, Race, and Tea Parties. The group hosts a radio show on BlogTalkRadio.com and has several videos posted on its blog.

Bureau of Indian Affairs (BIA)

Public Affairs Office, 1849 C Street NW
Washington, DC   20240
(202) 208-3711
e-mail: webmaster@bia.gov
website: www.bia.gov

The Bureau of Indian Affairs (BIA) handles the administration and management of 55.7 million acres of land held in trust by the United States for Native Americans. The federal agency provides education services to approximately forty-eight thousand Native American students, leases assets on Native American lands, directs agricultural programs, protects water and land rights, and maintains infrastructure and economic development. The BIA publishes the *American Indian Population and Labor Force Report* every two years.

Foundation for the American Indian

Box 267, 15 East Putnam Avenue, Greenwich, CT   06830
(203) 629-9030 • fax: (203) 629-9054
e-mail: info@foundationfortheamericanindian.org
website: www.foundationfortheamericanindian.org

The Foundation for the American Indian is committed to the enhancement of the quality of life of Native Americans through support for human services, economic development, the arts, education, and environmental stewardship. One of the foundation's projects is to develop wind energy projects for Native Americans. Its website contains information on this project among others.

Indian Gaming

Arrowpoint Media Inc., 14205 SE Thirty-Sixth Street
Suite 100, Bellevue, WA   98006
(425) 519-3710 • fax: (509) 891-0580
e-mail: info@indiangaming.com
website: www.indiangaming.com

Indian Gaming provides information about the Native American gaming industry, focusing primarily on promoting tourism to Native American casinos. Its magazine, *Indian Gaming*, is published monthly.

National Association of Tribal Historic Preservation Officers (NATHPO)

PO Box 19189, Washington, DC   20036-9189
(202) 628-8476 • fax: (202) 628-2241
e-mail: info@nathpo.org
website: www.nathpo.org

The National Association of Tribal Historic Preservation Officers (NATHPO) is a nonprofit organization made up of tribal government officials who are responsible for administering federal and tribal laws related to preservation. NATHPO provides support for its members' efforts to preserve, maintain, and promote Native American culture and traditions, work with federal land management agencies, and focus especially on promoting the Tribal Historic Preservation programs endorsed by the National Park Service.

National Congress of American Indians (NCAI)

1516 P Street NW, Washington, DC   20005
(202) 466-7767 • fax: (202) 466-7797
e-mail: ncai@ncai.org
website: www.ncai.org

The National Congress of American Indians (NCAI) works to inform the public and Congress about the governmental rights of Native Americans. Programs include promotion and support of education, enhancement of health care, and promotion of economic opportunity for Native Americans. The NCAI publishes materials on policy issues and has other resources through the NCAI Policy Research Center found on its website.

National Indian Gaming Association (NIGA)

224 Second Street SE, Washington, DC   20003

(202) 546-7711 • fax: (202) 546-1755

e-mail: info@indiangaming.org

website: www.indiangaming.org

The National Indian Gaming Association (NIGA) is a non-profit organization that works to protect and preserve the general welfare of tribes striving for self-sufficiency through gaming enterprises. NIGA works with the federal government and Congress to develop sound policies and practices and to provide technical assistance and advocacy on gaming-related issues. NIGA has a variety of publications related to gaming, including *Indian Gaming Law and Policy* and *2009 Economic Impact of Indian Gaming.*

National Indian Gaming Commission (NIGC)

1441 L Street NW, Suite 9100, Washington, DC   20005

(202) 632-7003 • fax: (202) 632-7066

e-mail: contactus@nigc.gov

website: www.nigc.gov

As an independent federal regulatory agency of the United States, the National Indian Gaming Commission (NIGC) was established pursuant to the Indian Gaming Regulatory Act of 1988. The commission is authorized to conduct investigations; undertake enforcement actions, including the issuance of notices of violation, assessment of civil fines, and/or issuance of closure orders; conduct audits; and review and approve tribal gaming ordinances. The agency publishes a number of reports on gaming revenue, compliance, and other topics.

National Museum of the American Indian (NMAI)

PO Box 23473, Washington, DC   20026-3473
(202) 633-1000
e-mail: nin@si.edu
website: www.nmai.si.edu

The National Museum of the American Indian (NMAI) is the sixteenth museum of the Smithsonian Institution and has three locations: the George Gustav Hey Center in New York City; the Cultural Resources Center in Suitland, Maryland; and the NMAI on the National Mall in Washington, DC. The museum works in collaboration with the Native peoples of the Western Hemisphere to protect and foster their cultures by re-affirming traditions and beliefs, encouraging contemporary artistic expression, and empowering the Indian voice. The museum publishes *American Indian* magazine, as well as an e-newsletter and several books.

National Tribal Environmental Council (NTEC)

4520 Montgomery Boulevard NE, Suite 3
Albuquerque, NM   87109
(505) 242-2175 • fax: (505) 242-2654
e-mail: info@ntec.org
website: www.ntec.org

The National Tribal Environmental Council (NTEC) is dedicated to working with and assisting tribes in the protection and preservation of tribal homelands. It provides several services, including national advocacy, a resource clearinghouse and reference library, and workshops on specific environmental issues. The NTEC also publishes the newsletter *Environmental Insights* several times each year.

Native American Emergency Relief

PO Box 1760, Temecula, CA   92593-1760
(951) 225-6700 • fax: (951) 225-6799
website: www.naerelief.org

The Native American Emergency Relief is a charitable aid program within World Emergency Relief (WER), which is made up of a global network of programs in twenty-four countries worldwide. WER focuses on providing critical resources and services for children, including water, food, health care, education, and safety, but also addresses the wider needs of families and communities.

Native American Rights Fund (NARF)
1506 Broadway, Boulder, CO   80302-6296
(303) 447-8760 • fax: (303) 443-7776
website: www.narf.org

The Native American Rights Fund (NARF) is a nonprofit organization that provides legal representation and technical assistance to Native American tribes, organizations, and individuals. It strives to ensure that national and state governments live up to their legal obligations; assists tribes in negotiating with individuals, companies, and governmental agencies; and helps draft and promote legislation favorable to Native Americans. The fund publishes the newsletter *Justice*, periodic legal reviews, case updates, and guides such as *Labor and Employment Law in Indian Country* and *A Practical Guide to the Indian Child Welfare Act*.

One Nation United
PO Box 3336, Redmond, WA   98073-3336
(206) 660-3085
e-mail: barb@onenationunited.org
website: www.onenationunited.org

One Nation United is a nonprofit organization working to change federal policies related to Native Americans. Some of the issues that One Nation United is concerned about are tribal sovereignty, the enforcement of treaty rights that affect private property rights, and creating a level playing field between tribal and nontribal businesses. One Nation United publishes the newsletter *One Nation United Update*.

Protect Sacred Sites
e-mail: Tamra@protectsacredsites.org
website: http://protectsacredsites.org

Protect Sacred Sites is a grassroots organization dedicated to the protection of sacred Native American lands, burial grounds, and artifacts from desecration or illegal sale and trade. The organization supports several tribes, government and state agencies, individual landowners, and environmental organizations. It works with Tribal Historic Preservation Officers to protest rights infringements and raise awareness of specific sites that are threatened or that have been desecrated and of violations of laws governing the proper handling of ancient Native American artifacts.

United States Commission on Civil Rights
624 Ninth Street NW, Washington, DC   20425
(202) 376-7700
e-mail: publications@usccr.gov
website: www.usccr.gov

The United States Commission on Civil Rights is the agency of the US government charged with investigating complaints of discrimination. In addition to investigating complaints, the commission collects information related to discrimination, appraises federal laws and policies with respect to discrimination, and submits recommendations to the president and Congress. It publishes the *Civil Rights Journal* and other publications, including *Broken Promises: Evaluating the Native American Health Care System* and *A Quiet Crisis: Federal Funding and Unmet Needs in Indian County.*

United States Senate Committee on Indian Affairs
838 Hart Office Building, Washington, DC   20510
(202) 224-2251
e-mail: comments@indian.senate.gov
website: www.indian.senate.gov

The United States Senate Committee on Indian Affairs has jurisdiction to study the unique problems of Native Americans and to propose legislation to alleviate these difficulties. Some of the issues of the committee are Native American education, economic development, land management, trust responsibilities, health care, and legal claims against the United States. Available at its website are recordings and transcripts of hearings, as well as other information about the issues being studied.

Bibliography of Books

Heather Burke et al., eds.
Kennewick Man: Perspectives on the Ancient One. Walnut Creek, CA: Left Coast Press, 2008.

Jeffrey R. Dudas
The Cultivation of Resentment: Treaty Rights and the New Right. Stanford, CA: Stanford University Press, 2008.

Laura E. Evans
Power from Powerlessness: Tribal Governments, Institutional Niches, and American Federalism. New York: Oxford University Press, 2011.

Jacqueline Fear-Segal
White Man's Club: Schools, Race, and the Struggle of Indian Acculturation. Lincoln: University of Nebraska Press, 2007.

Tom Flanagan, Christopher Alcantara, and André Le Dressay
Beyond the Indian Act: Restoring Aboriginal Property Rights. Montreal, Quebec: McGill-Queen's University Press, 2010.

Alexandra Harmon
Rich Indians: Native People and the Problem of Wealth in American History. Chapel Hill: University of North Carolina Press, 2010.

Alexandra Harmon, ed.
The Power of Promises: Rethinking Indian Treaties in the Pacific Northwest. Seattle: Center for the Study of the Pacific Northwest in association with University of Washington Press, 2008.

LaDonna Harris, Stephen M. Sachs, and Barbara Morris, eds. *Re-Creating the Circle: The Renewal of American Indian Self-Determination.* Albuquerque: University of New Mexico Press, 2011.

Eric C. Henson et al. *The State of the Native Nations: Conditions Under US Policies of Self-Determination.* New York: Oxford University Press, 2008.

Shari M. Huhndorf *Mapping the Americas: The Transnational Politics of Contemporary Native Culture.* Ithaca, NY: Cornell University Press, 2009.

Thomas W. Killion, ed. *Opening Archaeology: Repatriation's Impact on Contemporary Research and Practice.* Santa Fe, NM: School for Advanced Research Press, 2008.

Kenneth Lincoln, ed. *Gathering Native Scholars: UCLA's Forty Years of American Indian Culture and Research.* Los Angeles, CA: UCLA American Indian Studies Center, 2009.

Kenichi Matsui *Native Peoples and Water Rights: Irrigation, Dams, and the Law in Western Canada.* Montreal, Quebec: McGill-Queen's University Press, 2009.

Daniel McCool, Susan M. Olson, and Jennifer L. Robinson *Native Vote: American Indians, the Voting Rights Act, and the Right to Vote.* New York: Cambridge University Press, 2007.

Laughlin McDonald	*American Indians and the Fight for Equal Voting Rights.* Norman: University of Oklahoma Press, 2010.
Susan A. Miller and James Riding In, eds.	*Native Historians Write Back: Decolonizing American Indian History.* Lubbock, TX: Texas Tech University Press, 2011.
David J. Minderhout and Andrea T. Frantz	*Invisible Indians: Native Americans in Pennsylvania.* Youngstown, NY: Cambria Press, 2008.
Marianne O. Nielsen and Robert A. Silverman, eds.	*Criminal Justice in Native America.* Tucson: University of Arizona Press, 2009.
Alison Owings	*Indian Voices: Listening to Native Americans.* New Brunswick, NJ: Rutgers University Press, 2011.
Frank Pommersheim	*Broken Landscape: Indians, Indian Tribes, and the Constitution.* New York: Oxford University Press, 2009.
Justin B. Richland	*Arguing with Tradition: The Language of Law in Hopi Tribal Court.* Chicago, IL: University of Chicago Press, 2008.
Bradley G. Shreve	*Red Power Rising: The National Indian Youth Council and the Origins of Native Activism.* Norman: University of Oklahoma Press, 2011.
Andrea Smith	*Native Americans and the Christian Right: The Gendered Politics of Unlikely Alliances.* Durham, NC: Duke University Press, 2008.

George E. "Tink" Tinker — *American Indian Liberation: A Theology of Sovereignty*. Maryknoll, NY: Orbis Books, 2008.

Jace Weaver — *Notes from a Miner's Canary: Essays on the State of Native America*. Albuquerque: University of New Mexico Press, 2010.

David E. Wilkins, ed. — *The Hank Adams Reader: An Exemplary Native Activist and the Unleashing of Indigenous Sovereignty*. Golden, CO: Fulcrum Publishing, 2011.

Aleksandra Ziolkowska-Boehm — *Open Wounds: A Native American Heritage*. Pierpont, SD: Nemsi Books, 2009.

Index